LAND, PEOPLE & POLICY

The Problems & Techniques of Assembling Land for

the Urbanization of 100 Million New Americans

by

GORDON EDWARDS

Chandler-Davis Publishing Company
West Trenton, New Jersey 08628

TO MY BELOVED WIFE, SUZANNE

ACKNOWLEDGEMENTS

I wish to express my deep gratitude to all those who made this book possible. My research assistants, Dr. James Van de Water and Dr. Max Schlopy, worked many long and trying hours and performed masterfully under less than ideal conditions. Dr. George Randels accomplished the difficult task of proofreading and contributing to the substance of the work at the same time. My secretary, Mrs. Jean Cummings, performed far beyond the call of duty. I am particularly grateful to the President's Commission on Urban Problems, Senator Paul .Douglas, Chairman; for their generous assistance in helping me finance the basic research and travel.

Last, but certainly not least, I owe a lasting debt of thanks to my family. Without the love and encouragement of my wife Suzanne when the work became difficult, I could not have succeeded in completing the book.

Gordon Edwards

State University of New York at Buffalo
Buffalo, N.Y. 14214
February 14, 1969

PREFACE

The problems that grow out of the "ghettoization" of the cities are severe and self-reinforcing. Mass, unrelieved segregation means that effective community dialogue is cut off. Denied the traditional routes to effective political and economic power, the Negro is increasingly tempted to turn inward or to attract attention to his problems by violence.

It will take tremendous resources, imaginative new solutions, and effective political infighting to reverse present trends, or even to make a dent in them. There are, however, promising possibilities that we have not yet begun to tap. We could build New Towns in the outlying sections of our metropolitan regions with federal financial assistance and, therefore, with built-in requirements for housing lower-income groups and racial integration. If these new communities were attractive and the housing cost quite low, many white families might overcome their reluctance to live in mixed communities.

We could build "New Towns — in town" that would have greatly improved public services and facilities (good schools, in particular), exciting "lighted centers" for fun and shopping, intown industrial estates, and a great variety of housing. The creation of such communities would involve the application of the basic New Town principles to the gray areas of our cities.

The creation of such new communities should have as a prime objective the broadening of alternatives and the extension of diversity in urban life styles. In general, the alternatives available today make restrictiveness more attractive than openness, and community interaction a matter of crowding and annoyance, as in supermarkets and on superhighways.

— Harvey S. Perloff

Dean, School of Architecture & Urban Planning
University of California at Los Angeles

Contents

CHAPTER   **Page**

Preface by Harvey S. Perloff   v

1 INTRODUCTION   1
  Summary of Objectives   6
  Summary of Recommendations   8
  National Land Commission   8
  Regional Land Development Authorities   9
  Private Condemnation   10
  Land Purchase   10

2 LAND AND URBAN EXPANSION   13
  Past Urban Growth   13
  Future Metropolitan Growth   14
  Characteristics of Urban Growth   15
  The Pattern of Urban Growth   16
  What's Wrong With Urban Sprawl?   17
  The Need for Open Space   18
  Changing Concepts of Land Ownership   20
  National Policy on the Use of Urban Land   21

3 AN ANALYSIS: URBAN RENEWAL AND NEW TOWNS   29
  Urban Renewel and Rehabilitation   30
  The Relocation Problem   32
  Local Costs of the Program   33
  Finding a Developer   34
  A Look at Rehabilitation   35
  Urban Renewal and Rehabilitation in Summary   36
  The New Towns Concept   37
  The British New Towns   38
  The Swedish New Towns   40
  Finnish New Towns   40
  New Towns in the United States   41
  Problems of New Town Development   42

4 LAND ASSEMBLY: THE FOREIGN EXPERIENCE   47
  England   48
  Norway   54
  Sweden   58
  Finland   64
  Belgium   66
  The Netherlands   68
  Puerto Rico   72

5 THE EFFECT OF TECHNOLOGY AND DESIGN ON
  LAND COSTS, UTILIZATION AND ASSEMBLY   77
  Economies of Sale   77
  Technology   80
  Site Planning and Open Space   82

Planned Unit Development   82
Design, People and Cars   84
Demand Management   85
Rising Expectations   88
In Summary   91

6 PROBLEMS OF LAND ASSEMBLY 94
In-City Land Assembly   94
Land in the Marketplace   94
Assembly Under Urban Renewal Programs   97
Suburban Land Assembly   100
Governmental Frictions in Suburban Assembly   104
Summary   106

7 RECOMMENDATIONS: HOW WE MIGHT IMPLEMENT
OUR NATIONAL POLICIES   110
The National Land Commission   110
Structure, Functions and Activities   111
Comparison with British Land Commission   113
The Regional Land Development Authority   114
Structure, Functions and Activities   116
Private Condemnation   119
Commentary on Private Condemnation   120
Land Costs   122
Relocation   122
Land Purchase Program   122
Existing Land Purchase Programs   124
Implementation of a Land Purchase Program   126
Recommended: A Comprehensive Program   131
What Would an Effective Land Assembly Program Cost?   133

8 POLITICAL IMPLEMENTATION 138
Overcoming Inertia   138
Professional Shortcomings   139
Oblivion in the Old-Line Agencies   141
Formulation of Policy   144
U.S.-Canadian Commission Reports   145
Kaiser Committee Recommendation   147
Author's Commentary   149

9 CONCLUSION   152

INDEX   156

AUTHOR'S FOREWORD

More and more people are crowding onto less and less land. The competition for land in our great urban belts is increasing at startling rates. The land and water resources available for highways, shopping centers, subdivisions and jetports around and between major metropolitan areas are not expandable. The last open land between Baltimore and Washington is rapidly disappearing. The real estate agents from Detroit are tripping over the developers from Chicago. Land prices in the California urban belt have doubled and tripled in the past ten years. The crunch comes when we have totally polluted our existing resources of land and water. The shape of our urban future is cast, but it is not too late to plan for the best use of our dwindling resources. Meanwhile, we must also find ways to unlock the ghetto by building low-income housing in suburbs and beyond and rebuilding slum areas.

This book proposes a practical and realistic method of using governmental powers of eminent domain, combined with private capital and managerial skills, to help solve the urban crisis, conserve our shrinking resources and build a better urban America.

Chapter 1

INTRODUCTION

The urban crisis has become a national crisis, our number one problem. The very phrase "urban crisis" has become a signal for action, calling forth a host of action programs designed to solve the problems of the cities — Model Cities, urban coalitions and urban institutes. The specter of crisis is stalking the land, burning the cities, and threatening families. It demands a swift and effective response. We seek the magic bullets which will vanquish the werewolves and vampires that destroy cities. The programs or magic bullets of politicians and intellectuals alike have been rich in rhetoric but short on money.

The fact is, of course, that there are no magic bullets. Contrary to the empty promises of Conservatives and Liberals alike, it will take much more money, both public and private, and much better management of future urban investments. As Joseph Block, chairman of Inland Steel put it, "If you really want to solve the problems of the inner cities, the only answer remains big amounts of tax dollars. Sure, private industry can do some things, but the government must be the prime mover."[1] In short, it will be a long, hard, uphill struggle to find not *the* solution but rather many solutions to our urban problems.

There is also a need to "sort out" our urban problems, to identify appropriate areas and levels of responsibility. Every problem from poverty to pollution comes under the heading of urban problems. As Daniel P. (Pat) Moynihan, President

1

Nixon's chief urbanologist and the Executive Secretary of the newly-created Council for Urban Affairs points out, the industrialist who pollutes the air has little in common with the welfare child living in the ghetto yet both are included under the rubric of "urban problems."

Too many problems have been called urban. Those of rural migrants to urban slums are national in scope, involving such factors as the mechanization of agriculture which pushes people off farms and the disparity in state welfare programs which in turn pull the poor into ghettos. This is one of the root causes of mounting "social dynamite" in the cities, yet it involves agricultural policies, private industry and state and federal welfare policies. Obviously, more than discrete urban problems are at work here. National policies that encourage or decelerate economic expansion, employment, and other economic phenomena are also at work. At present many of our policies, like welfare, frustrate urban reformers. They might be labeled anti-urban strategies. Yet failure to adopt positive effective policies is also a strategy. It may not be a successful one but it nevertheless is an expression of society's commitment to the urban problem.

In order to bring about long-term solutions to the urban crisis, new concepts and programs will have to be devised to implement new policies. That's what this book is all about — the question of our national land policies (or non-policies) and some suggested changes pointing toward the kinds of policies and programs we need in the urban age.

Twenty years ago our political leaders hailed the new urban renewal legislation by saying that our goal was no slums in twenty years.[2] Today we find such statements cynically amusing. The slums of Chicago, New York, Cleveland, Los Angeles and most other large metropolitan areas are bigger than ever. Yet, in that same twenty years, Oslo, Stockholm, Helsinki and Amsterdam have managed to eliminate their slums and build well-ordered suburbs. In terms of quality of urban life, the United States is rapidly becoming a second-rate power. The message is there for everyone to read. The quality of our urban environment grows steadily worse; first, because we do not have a proper urban policy; and second, we do not have an adequate planning policy. We have transportation policies, housing policies and economic policies; agricultural policies and public land policies. These policies are the potential muscles of significant development, but they are un-coordinated. No one is capable of flexing them in unison. Everyone is in charge of policy, yet no one is in charge.

No single agency in the national government has a clear assignment to develop national economic development and urbanization policy and goals. The current public debate about what is variously called "urban-rural balance," "balanced economic development," or "balanced urbanization" highlights the need for the establishment of a national planning process which can provide the framework within which relevant policy issues can be decided.

The activities of virtually all of the major Federal departments and agencies directly influence national economic development and urbanization:

> Those of the Department of Housing and Urban Development are almost exclusively concerned with urbanization.

> Transportation facilities are one of the key determinants of economic activity and urban growth, and the Department of Transportation's programs and policies have a major impact on where growth takes place and on the economic stability of regions.

> The Economic Development Administration in the Department of Commerce, operating under the Public Works and Economic Development Act of 1965, is directly concerned with economically depressed regions.

> The Department of Agriculture is increasingly concerned with the economic status of depressed rural areas.

> The utilization of public lands under the jurisdiction of the Department of Interior can also have significant impact on urbanization patterns, both by the release of reclassified surplus land for urban development and by providing recreational and open space facilities for urban concentrations. The availability of a host of services assisted under the programs of the Department of Health, Education and Welfare can also fundamentally affect where urban growth takes place.[3]

In addition to muscular coordination we need some new land

assembly muscles, to help us achieve what others have managed to achieve — a decent urban environment.

In our continuing shift from a rural to an urban nation, we have come to the crossroads in the use of our country's urban land resources. The time has passed when we can squander our heritage with impunity. As Thomas Jefferson once observed, "The earth is given as a common stock for men to labor and live on." Today that stock is nearing depletion. We can no longer afford the haphazard development and land pollution which has characterized the growth of our urban areas. We can no longer afford the high cost of urban sprawl.

Our Constitution makes no reference to urban land policy. When it was drawn up, only five percent of the population was urban. It was a widely scattered population of less than four million. Today we have a population of over 200 million which is 70% urban. By the year 2000 we will have 300 million people, 90% urban, living on less than 10% of our land.

The issue today is not merely land, but rather urban land: land strategically located to meet the needs of the people, land for homes, for recreation, for cultural and economic development. Land is a basic ingredient in the growth of our nation and in the happiness and welfare of its people. Urban development must be planned and regulated to insure the most efficient use of our urban land resources. One of the crucial elements in effective land use planning is the assembly of land for both public and private large-scale development.

This book is addressed to the problem of assembling land to provide for our open space, recreational and housing needs. In his 1968 State of the Union Message, President Johnson said the nation badly needed six million new housing units built over the next ten years.[4] In his 1969 message he reaffirmed this goal and called for 300,000 new, low and middle-income housing starts by 1970.[5] The goals set by Congress in the Omnibus Housing Act of 1968 were based more on need than on what could be accomplished. The Act called for six million low-cost units over the next 10 years; 300,000 for the current year. It is also significant that President Johnson, in his 1969 message to Congress, restated his appeal for the creation of New

Communities to complement our efforts to revitalize the inner city.

The new Republican secretary of HUD, George M. Romney, conceded that the nation surely needed the new housing but claimed the goal was "unrealistic" because there wasn't enough money.[6] The point is that, regardless of the ebb and flow of political tides, some 500,000 new housing units are needed immediately and six million units will be needed in the 1970's. If these new homes are to be built in a more attractive and economically efficient urban environment, it is essential that we find new methods and techniques of guiding urban development and assembling land for well planned new communities.

Even more important. these new methods and techniques must maximize the initiative and genius of private industry for three reasons. First, government can't do the job alone. The traditional function of industry is to produce, distribute and sell goods, including housing. Big business has performed this function better than other sectors have performed theirs. Second, no one wants government to take over all the functions of city building. Indeed, many think we should return many more functions to the private sector. Third, there is an emerging awareness of business's responsibilities to the city, not because of a vague "social awareness" but rather a realization of the urban crisis as a threat to existing investments in cities along with the opportunities for creating new markets among the emerging poor.

The proposed Land Assembly program relies on a combination of governmental powers (primarily eminent domain) and private capital. Perhaps most important for political success is the fact that this is one new program which would not require astronomical amounts of tax dollars to implement. Rather, it attempts to make maximum use of the new business doctrine of socio-commercial enterprise as proposed by one of our leading bankers, George Champion: "Business must move from the defensive to the offensive and begin pushing the boundary line between the public and private sectors the other way. Both business and society stand to gain from the doctrine of socio-commercial enterprise."[7]

5

Private industry can be attracted to the great task of building new towns and rebuilding old cities, but it is the function of leadership, both public and private, to structure the ways and means of enticing business and industry to finance and build the new urban America. Businessman Eli Goldston, President of Eastern Gas and Fuel Associates, has identified four "economic carrots that may hasten business entry into public problems . . . all designed to compensate for conditions which otherwise would make reasonable profit unlikely:"[8] (1) guarantees and insurances (2) tax benefits (3) subsidies, and (4) contracts and franchises.[9]

All four devices are necessary components if we are to achieve realistic "participation" on the part of big business. Particularly essential are subsidies and tax benefits relating to the "front money" necessary to cover the extended lead-time which is implicit in the construction of whole new towns.

Perhaps the unique contribution of this book is to suggest the adding of governmental legal powers for "Land Assembly" to the growing list of incentives and controls that will attract private industry to come to grips with the practical realities of community building and renewal. The communities we see around us today, both rich and poor, were built, for better or worse, by private industry largely through the private decision-making process. If the community-building process is going to be turned around and made more responsive to public needs, particularly in terms of housing the poor, it will turn on the profit motive and not on moral exhortation from political leaders. Rather, our political leaders must re-structure governmental powers (such as eminent domain) and provide great sums of money to attract the private sectors into far greater participation in the urban environment business.

Summary of Objectives

About the only thing urbanologists, both as planners and politicians, can agree on is that problems of cities and urban development are broad, deep and wonderously complicated and that government alone cannot solve them. Further, it will take a combination or "coalition" of government, business, industry, labor, universities, foundations and almost everyone else to find appropriate solutions. Yet, who can lead the coalition? In this light, the objectives of this book are remarkably realistic and manageable. They have been tried and found workable in other post-industrial societies. Moreover, the time may be right for realistic urban goals. As management expert Peter F. Drucker pointed out in his penetrating article, The Sickness of Government, " . . . government may shed the megalomania that now obsesses it and learn how to confine itself to realistic goals."[10] They deal with the basic component of urban growth, land; how it is used and misused, and how we, as a nation, can do a better job of land management in the future than we have in the past. The objectives simply stated are:

1. To analyze urban growth trends and the need for programs of land assembly to provide for well planned urban development, both in-city and in suburban and rural areas;

2. To analyze specific problems of the assembling of land for urban uses by private developers, including costs due to holdouts and carrying charges, the effect of slum areas and fragmented land ownership on redevelopment and the extent to which problems of land assembly contribute to inefficient and unattractive metropolitan development;

3. To analyze techniques and procedures used by public agencies and private developers in (a) central city land assembly for urban renewal and downtown redevelopment, and (b) suburban and rural land assembly for new communities;

4. To describe techniques and procedures for land acquisition, compensation and disposition used in various foreign countries, and to evaluate their potential for meeting future problems of land assembly in this country;

5. To recommend public programs designed to assist the private developer in acquiring land of suitable size and location for private redevelopment in cities;

6. To recommend public programs designed to assist the private developer in acquiring land for the development of well planned new communities, both in the city and in suburban areas;

7. To recommend public programs designed to purchase land and development rights in suburban and rural areas to insure well planned urban development in accordance with regional and local planning programs.

7

Summary of Recommendations

This book recommends land assembly programs in suburban, rural and central city areas. It calls for positive action rather than more urban distress signals and intellectual hand-wringing. The recommended land assembly programs and techniques could be carried forward in suburban and rural areas, independent of programs for land assembly in the central city. But, because of the need to rebuild our cities, it is recommended that programs for land assembly be initiated in the city as well as in the suburbs and the open countryside surrounding our metropolitan areas.

The recommended program is composed of four key elements; (1) a National Land Commission, (2) Regional Land Development Authorities, (3) Private Condemnation and (4) Land Purchase Program. It cuts across federal, state and local levels of government and relies on private initiative to get efficiently planned urban development under way at an early date.

1. National Land Commission

While all power and decision-making responsibility would be decentralized, a National Land Commission is needed to encourage and promote regional land policies designed to insure the orderly and efficient development of urban land. Further, since the federal government is a great land owner, the proposal would coordinate land acquisition, disposal and development programs at federal levels. Conflicting objectives, interests and programs of federal agencies could be harmonized with local plans. The growth of urban America might then proceed in a bit more rational way and perhaps make more efficient use of urban land — a limited resource. A single agency at the national level, independent of other federal agencies, is needed because the problems of urban development are national in scope. They cross state boundaries and the states have a vital role to play, but 50 separate policies will not do the job. The Land Commission should have autonomy and it should be independent. In effect, it must be a single-purpose agency. The primary thrust must be the efficient use of our urban land resources so that it can deal with land policy issues across the board rather than from the biased single-purpose objectives of highways, hospitals, airports, open space, housing, or defense installations.

To meet these objectives the National Land Commission would be empowered by Congress:

(a) To assist the state governments in the establishment of Regional Land Development Authorities, and to provide financial assistance to state governments for the establishment of these authorities;

(b) To establish criteria for the structure and jurisdiction of Regional Land Development Authorities;

(c) To provide funds to the Regional Authorities for the purchase of land and other property rights. The National Land Commission will provide regional land development authorities with funds for the purchase of lease-holds and development rights;

(d) To approve the annual programs of each Regional Land Development Authority and provide the initial funding needed for these programs;

(e) To coordinate urban land acquisition and disposal by other federal departments or agencies;

(f) To coordinate land acquisition and disposal by state and local governmental agencies.

2. Regional* Land Development Authorities

Regional Land Development Authorities must be created by the state or states in which they will function. State participation is essential.

(a) Members of the Authority will be appointed by the state and will include representatives of state, regional and local governments and planning organizations;

(b) The Authority must be given the power of eminent domain under a procedure designed to facilitate the rapid assembly of land;

---

*For the purpose of this study, the word "regional" is defined to include, as a minimum, the geographic extent of the Standard Metropolitan Statistical Area (SMSA). In those areas where the SMSA or other factors indicate that the authority should include parts of more than one state, the development of interstate compacts, similar to the Port of New York Authority, would be encouraged.

(c) The Authority must be given the power to overrule local land use controls which conflict with metropolitan and regional needs.

The functions of the Regional Land Development Authority will include:

(a) The purchase of land or property rights in urban or exurban land in accordance with a comprehensive land purchase program;

(b) The assembly of land designated by private developers for projects approved by the Authority;

(c) The coordination of land acquisition and disposal by federal, state and local governmental agencies within its region.

3. Private Condemnation

Large scale development requires a condemnation device which will permit the private developer to choose precisely those properties which he wants to improve. Under this device, the developer will prepare a detailed and comprehensive plan of any areas he proposes to develop. This plan, together with a bid price for the property involved, will be submitted to the Regional Land Development Authority. The Authority will make a preliminary determination regarding the feasibility of the proposal; if favorable, it will then provide for public hearings and other investigatory procedures on which a final decision will be based. If approved, a contract defining the responsibilities of both the developer and the Authority will be prepared. The Authority shall begin condemnation proceedings immediately, under a new streamlined procedure. Title to the condemned properties will vest in the Authority upon the filling of the plan. The developer may acquire an automatic right-of-entry at that time, with formal transfer of title occuring later according to the contract terms.

The "in-city" developer is often frustrated in his attempts to assemble land. Many small parcels are involved. Holdouts refuse to sell. The time and expense involved in overcoming these problems are prohibitive. Private condemnation will remedy this situation.

4. Land Purchase

There are two basic objectives of a land purchase program. First, it provides an effective land use planning tool to control urban development. Second, it provides land for our open space and recreational needs. It is essential that the program be tailored to meet the specific needs of each area or region. The Regional Authority must be empowered to use a broad range of techniques, including the purchase and disposal of land, leases and other property rights, to accomplish its individual objectives. The advantages of local experimentation and adjustment that have accrued to our decentralized form of government must be retained in the implementation of this program.

An effective land purchase program must include the purchase of vacant land in the central city area. This land could be used for parks, playgrounds and other recreational activities, or it could be held by the Authority and developed under a lease until such time as someone wished to purchase the land. This phase of the program would have to be somewhat restricted, however, due to the political implications of removing land from the city's tax base.

The second phase would involve an extensive purchase and purchase-leaseback program on the immediate urban fringe. The principal objective of this activity would be the prevention of urban sprawl and the control of immediate urban development. It would have the positive effect of easing the problem of land assembly for both the private developer and public agencies. The delay involved in condemnation proceedings would be substantially reduced. The leases could be either long or short term and would embody such restrictions as the Authority deems desirable in view of local and regional plans. The Authority would also purchase land in suburban areas to be donated to local governments for regional and local open space and recreational needs.

The third and most important phase of this program would be the purchase of development rights in rural areas. This phase of the program is designed to control long range development and land assembly problems. Implementation will usually involve the negotiated purchase of such rights in the marketplace. Condemnation procedures will be available when absolutely necessary. The purchase of development rights will result in substantial cost savings over a full-title acquisition program.

11

references/footnotes

[1] Block, as quoted in an article by Allan T. Demaree, entitled, "What Business Wants from President Nixon," *Fortune* (February 1969), p. 87.

[2] The preamble of the Housing Act of 1949 promises " . . . the realization as soon as feasible of the goal of a decent home and suitable living environment for every American family . . . . "

[3] Advisory Commission on Intergovernmental Relations, Washington, D.C., April 1968, A-32, *Urban and Rural America: Policies for Future Growth,* pp. 132-33.

[4] President Johnson's State Of the Union Message, *New York Times,* January 18, 1968, p. 16: " . . . industry and labor, to start building 300,000 housing units for low and middle-income families next year — three times more than this year. We must make it possible for thousands of families to become homeowners, not rent-payers. I propose, for the consideration of this Congress, a 10-year campaign to build six million new housing units for low and middle-income families."

[5] President Johnson's Message to Congress, *New York Times,* January 16, 1969. "The 1968 Act will involve the Federal Government in a new and closer partnership with private industry and labor to provide 26 million new or rehabilitated homes and apartments over the next 10 years. A significant part of this new program will be Federal assistance for 6 million dwelling units to assure adequate housing for families with meager resources. The initial goal is to build or repair 700,000 homes and apartments for low and moderate-income urban and rural families in the first 2 years, (including approximately 300,000 by 1970)."

[6] Romney, as quoted in an article by John Herbers, entitled, "Romney Reports Review of Policy," *New York Times*, February 5, 1969, p. 23.

[7] Champion, "Creative Competition," *Harvard Business Review* (May-June 1967), p. 671.

[8] Goldston, "New Prospects for American Business," *Daedalus* (Winter 1969), p. 90.

[9] *Ibid.,* pp. 90-91.

[10] Drucker, "The Sickness of Government," *The Public Interest* (Winter 1969), p. 12.

Chapter 2

LAND AND URBAN EXPANSION

Past Urban Growth

Public attitudes regarding the proper use of land are made up of ethical, philosophical, social and economic myths and beliefs about the true purpose of the land. But it is historical development that remains the single most important factor in determining the public attitude.

Our Nation was born rural, with a fantastic abundance of land. In 1690, the North American Colonies had a total "urban" population of some 17,700 people. Most of the urbanites were located in five small towns: Boston, Philadelphia, New York, Newport and Charles Town. Within two generations the towns grew into small cities. But, while these cities continued to grow, the public attitude toward urbanization remained essentially negative. Cities were held in low esteem. Thomas Jefferson regarded them as a cancer on the body politic.[11]

This national contempt for cities, urban values and the character of urban growth continued into the 19th Century where policies and programs were designed to exploit the land-rich "West." With the Homestead Act of 1862, we gave 160 acres to anyone who would settle on it and make improvements to it. Land was given to the new states, and to private railroads as well. Towns sprang up along the railroad rights-of-way, and land speculation was widespread.[12] Throughout this period there was little public concern with the use or misuse of urban land. The public attitude toward land was that we were a land-rich nation and God made it thus for man's exploitation and profit.

It was the rapid industrialization and urbanization of the Twentieth Century that forced the nation to turn its attention to the city. The need for controlling urban land uses was recognized early, but little was actually done. The more comfortable concept of land use for profit and exploitation was firmly entrenched in the popular ethic and the law. More and more land was plowed over, built on and otherwise urbanized. In 1900, cities occupied some six million acres; by 1950, this figure had grown to 17 million acres, and by 1962, 27.2 million acres was urbanized.[13] According to UN demographers, three of the nine largest "urban agglomerations" in the world are in the U.S. The list includes New York with 11.3 million people; Tokyo, 10.5 million; London, 7.5 million; Paris, 7.4 million; Buenos Aires, 7 million; Shanghai, 6.9 million; Los Angeles, 6.8 million; Chicago, 6.6 million; and Moscow, 6.5 million.[14] As impressive as this past growth appears, the great urban push across the landscape remains before us.

Future Metropolitan Growth

By the year 2000 the nation will add over 100 million to our present urban population of approximately 115 million.[15] Within the next two generations our three largest urban regions will contain over one-half of the total population of the United States. Dr. Jerome Pickard has defined these regions as Atlantic seaboard, Lower Great Lakes and California. Kahn & Wiener have termed them "Boswash," "Chipitts," and "Sansan."[16] Boswash identifies the megalopolis that will extend from Boston to Washington, and will contain about 80 million people, almost one-quarter of the projected American population. Chipitts, concentrated around the Great Lakes, may stretch from Chicago to Pittsburgh and north to Canada, including Detroit, Toledo, Cleveland, Akron, Buffalo and Rochester. This conurbation seems likely to contain more than one-eighth of our population. Sansan, a Pacific urban region that will stretch from San Francisco to San Diego, will contain approximately one-tenth of the nation's population or some 25 million people.

What form will the future push of urbanization take? According to Dr. Robert E. Dickinson, by the year 2000 the Atlantic seaboard megalopolis will push "westward through

14

central New York State and Pennsylvania to the Middle Western states as far as the Mississippi, and beyond the southern fringe into Kentucky and Tennessee.[17] The groups of cities in the southeastern states do not form a continuous belt, but the closeness of these lesser clusters indicates that they make up one of the major urban regions of the nation. The Los Angeles and San Francisco regions are rapidly spreading into central California. Houston-Galveston and New Orleans are extending tentacles toward each other, and will soon merge. Seattle-Tacoma and Portland are substantial in size, but though functionally interrelated, they are still widely separated. These areas indicate the outer framework within which the urban growth of the next few decades will take place.[18]

Characteristics of Urban Growth

The urban regions of America will continue to grow in size and economic importance. But what is the nature of this urban expansion? Across the country, urban growth has been occurring primarily in the suburbs. Between 1950 and 1960 our central cities increased their populations by only 1.5 percent, while metropolitan rings more than doubled (62 percent increase). Many cities showed an absolute decline in population.[19] In 1956, three-quarters of the dwelling units in major metropolitan areas, measured by number or value, were built outside the central city.[20] Even more significantly, our national highway building program brought more land within reach of the city, within the radius of thirty or forty minutes; a time-distance factor which most people seem willing to spend in going to and from work.[21]

Increased accessibility brought business and industry into the suburbs. Business and industry located in obsolete, inefficient plants found their market positions weakened by competitors using new production technologies which require single story plants and more land for horizontal expansion. The cost and delay of land assembly in the city were also factors in the shift to the suburbs. "In the central city, plant expansion frequently entails complicated, time consuming and costly assembly of land, clearance and reconstruction of plant."[22] Boston's circumferential Route 128 provides a dramatic example of industrial firms moving to outlying areas for modernization or

15

expansion programs. Highways encircling Philadelphia, Baltimore and Washington provide similar experiences.

The Pattern of Urban Growth

The character of urbanization has been widely criticized as casual, sporadic and haphazard, resulting in complex problems at every level of government. Disfunctional urban patterns also create costly problems for the private sector. Slums and blight have engulfed large portions of our major cities. Our cities are characterized by social violence, obsolescence, pollution, poor schools and traffic congestion. In the suburbs we find rising taxes, chaotic land use patterns, strip commercial development and inadequate parks and open space.

The suburbs of yesterday, the so-called "gray areas," are rapidly becoming the slums of today as the social and economic ills of the city push outward to consume ever larger areas. Beyond the suburbs, prime agricultural land gives way to scattered ribbons of homes and businesses, stretching finger-like along rural roadways and country lanes. The late Hugh Pomeroy, for years the planning director of Westchester County, N.Y., referred to this landscape pollution as "terricide." Non-planning permits the by-passing of land, and the stringing out of sewer and other utilities in a most expensive and inefficient way.

There are many factors which contribute to this "urban sprawl." One of these is the high cost of in-city land. Developers are forced to "leapfrog" over expensive, close-in land, to less expensive, far-out land. However, the cost of land is not the only contributing factor to urban sprawl. Large tracts of land are not available in the city, or on the immediate urban fringe. In addition, in-city land is built up. All too often, the cost of preparing such built up land for new development is higher than the cost of developing vacant land. [23]

Los Angeles has been maligned around the world as a swinging example of sprawl. Its six and one-half million people were spread over 1400 square miles in 1960. This pattern is also found in other major western cities such as Dallas-Fort Worth, Kansas City, Phoenix, San Diego and Albuquerque. [24] All the observers of the urban scene predict that, without major policy changes and more effective land use control devices, sprawl will be the pattern of the future.

What's Wrong with Urban Sprawl?

The problem is not shortage of land. America's 1.9 billion acres will provide sufficient land for several centuries of urban growth. However, empty land in Oregon is not going to help the man in Paterson, New Jersey. Within the limits of our major metropolitan areas, there is a surprising amount of empty land due to leapfrogging. But it is scattered — a vacant lot here and there — with no single parcel large enough to be of much use.[25]

In controversies over land use planning and development, the cry of "leapfrogging" is often heard. This refers to the leapfrogging of development over potential building sites into the unspoiled countryside. Upon closer examination economists have determined that it is a rational phenomenon of the market. There is a tendency for landowners near the cutting edge of urban developments to have optimistic expectations about the value of their land. Such owners have a tendency to hold out for higher prices which they are constantly adjusting upward because they feel that the ever-increasing accessibility to the center of urbanization enhances its value. The leapfrogging developer's response is rational. In order to drive down the cost of development, he "leaps" over more expensive land in search of cheaper land which he can process into a salable product, homes for lower prices. In the American ethos, the consumer wants more land for less money and is willing to drive a bit further to achieve it, particularly where expressways and freeways are available to maximize his automobility.

There are two dominant schools of thought on the subject of urban sprawl, and both are emotionally charged. The first view is that it wreaks havoc upon the countryside, destroying our natural heritage of field and stream. The other view holds that it is a matter of individual initiative to exploit the countryside and transform land into a useful economic commodity, thus increasing the value of the land by building new homes for growing families and adding to the gross national product. Both views are equally valid because we do not have a policy to deal

17

with the future of urban America. In other words, all of the many public interests, particularly those of the taxpayer and future residents, have not been taken into account. The argument is determined by the narrow interest of the developers on the one hand and conservationists on the other. The developer usually wins. The public interest must take a broader view that it is not simply the exploitation of land but rather the coordination of highways, water, sewers, parks and recreation that is important here. Coordination of such services requires planning in advance of development.

Since the urban crisis is now a national problem, we must begin at the highest policy level in the land. The United States, among the major industrialized and urbanized nations, is the only one which has failed to develop a national urban land policy, and the quality of urban environment of both cities and suburbs reflects a history of lack of concern. The argument that, unlike Holland or Sweden, we are land rich and do not need to worry is meaningless when we put the scope of urban expansion in perspective. Over the next three decades, when a national policy would be in effect, our nation will become 90% urbanized. We will add 100 million new people and we will build as many houses, stores and highways as we have built in our entire history. The mind boggles, yet the alternatives and the consequences of continued drift are clear. Our failures will continue to spill across the countryside — the evidence of shabby roadside development and the high cost of public services are there for everyone to see and pay for. Our lack of policy has resulted in the worst of both possible worlds, bad esthetics and bad economics.

The Need for Open Space*

Open space has many uses: recreation and ecological protection of water basins, shorelines, lakes, forest and wildlife preserves. Unfortunately, the fact is that land around our metropolitan areas is being urbanized at the rate of

---

* For the purposes of this book, open space means functional open space in public or private hands serving a public purpose.

approximately one-half million acres annually, with little guidance or control. Open space needs are often neglected.

New land conservation policies must be formulated in order to achieve a positive approach to land development. "As with our traditional resources, we must see our 'new' resources — the urban land, the open space, the air above us, and the urban waterways — as integral parts of our national wealth."[26] The need for preserving open space is clear. It is particularly important in new residential development. Water-courses, rock out-croppings and trees must be preserved to enhance the natural beauty of our urban areas.

As our population pushes toward 300 million by the year 2000, it grows more affluent and has a wider range of recreational needs. We are in danger of losing unique and irreplaceable features of the landscape, particularly our shorelines, lakes, rivers and marshes that remain unpolluted. Clearly, our seashores are a magnificent national heritage which merit protection and preservation, yet they are being lost at a phenomenal rate.

In November, 1968, the voters of Oregon turned down a proposed bond issue to preserve their splendid coastline, largely for reasons of economy. That coastline, like others, is a national treasure which will increase in value over the years. The time has come when the Federal Government should acquire all the seacoasts of the nation. As we saw in the section on the future of metropolitan growth, the East Coast, West Coast and Gulf Coast are precisely where most of the future urbanization will occur. Moreover, with the rapidly increasing consumption of second homes, motels and resorts, our coastline is in danger of disappearing behind walls of private compounds available only to the well-to-do, with the less fortunate relegated to over-crowded public parks. With public ownership we must also recognize the economic implications of private development of our seashore and permit private lease-holds of coastal properties. Federal, state and local governments should acquire title to our coastline, supervise it and work to insure that the development will be well planned and managed so that it adds to the national estate rather than the billboard jungle. The land assembly policies, programs and techniques proposed here will be of extreme importance in acquiring and developing open space in the urban setting.

Changing Concepts of Land Ownership

Many studies have been made of the problems of our urban development. They suggest methods to control and guide urbanization. These efforts are not sufficient. We must re-evaluate some of the basic concepts which govern our urban life. One concept we must re-evaluate is land ownership. The basic issue is who should own urban land and what rights in urban land should the owner possess?[27]

Throughout history, land ownership has been closely associated with political and economic power. In this country, democracy began as a system which gave the vote to him who had proven his worth by becoming a landowner. There were very few restrictions on his "right" to do whatever he wanted with the land he owned. Our concept of land ownership was governed by the belief that the best interests of society would be served if each individual land owner had maximum freedom.

Land ownership is a concept based on a complex legal system deliberately constructed by society. The function of the property concept is to regulate ownership in the best interests of society as a whole.[28] "The basic question is, what institution or system of land control best serves the common good?"[29]

In early American history we encouraged the development of frontier land by private interests. We did this by guaranteeing and protecting their rights in the land that they acquired and developed. This early concept of land ownership served the best interests of society at that time.

The impact of Twentieth Century industrialization and urbanization demands a new concept of land ownership. Our present system of land use controls still maximizes individual freedom. In recent years we have seen greater restrictions in the form of zoning, subdivision regulations, and other government intervention, but the freedom of private landowners is still a sacred cow. The time has come to make a crucial decision. Do the demands of our society now require urban land to be treated

20

as a community resource? Do we need a national policy on the use of urban land? What concept of land ownership will best help us to rebuild our cities and guide future urban growth?

National Policy on the Use of Urban Land

For far too many years we have tried to deal with our crisis in land and urban expansion on a "crash basis," rather than by long range planning. As experts have said, "We can no longer afford this seat-of-the-pants approach."[30]

Time and time again politicians, planners and conservationists have called for a national policy for urban land use. As William L. Slayton, executive vice-president of Urban America Inc., expressed it, "I think it is time that we established a national policy for dealing with urbanization."[31]

Democratic Senator Edward M. Kennedy and Republican Senator Charles Percy have also identified the need for new land policies. In December of 1967, Agriculture Secretary Orville L. Freeman sponsored a great national conference at the State Department in Washington, D.C., on "National Growth and its Distribution." Distinguished speakers such as the Vice-President, the secretaries of HEW, Labor and HUD cried the need for a national urban policy. The Vice-President said, "We need a far-reaching national policy on urbanization and the machinery to implement it."[32]

A year later in January 1969, Secretary Freeman provided ad hoc national policy by backing the development of a black new town to be built in North Carolina by Floyd B. McKissick Enterprises. The secretary promised his department's ". . . complete support in planning and developing the community." The secretary went on to say that ". . . it was perfect nonsense to ignore the countryside and huddle ourselves in less and less space."[33] In addition, the Nixon Administration "promised continuing support," according to McKissick.[34]

The new town, to be called "Soul City," would be built, owned and occupied by Negroes. It is planned for a population of 18,000. Mr. McKissick said, ". . . Soul City would be aimed primarily at offering urban job opportunities for black people but would be open to all races." The integrationist, indeed every

American concerned with justice and the future survival of the nation, might well applaud Mr. McKissick's goal. On the other hand a more careful analysis of white racism might lead to a new and different set of urban policies. White choice of neighborhoods is probably not dependent on maintaining "ethnic purity." The objective, rather, is a vague but deep-seated emotional concern with what sociologists call "cultural dominance." The American white middle class, like the middle class in any country "... want to be sure that the social, cultural, and economic milieu and values of their own group dominate their own residential environment and the educational environment of their children."[35] The point is that class rather than color is probably the critical factor in "white racism" and the resulting black ghetto, and the trap — the American dilemma — is that the vast majority of middle-class white Americans confuse color with class and choose their neighborhoods and associates accordingly. This "law of dominance" is a critical factor in developing a national urban land policy. As more black families seek a wider range of housing choices, better job opportunities and improved education for their children, land must be made available for low income housing in many new communities around the metropolitan area, as well as assurance of open occupancy for the black middle-class. In the long run, the integrated dispersal of the ghetto is probably our most important national urban goal. Meanwhile short run improvements of ghetto conditions, or enrichment through Model Cities-type programs, are also essential.

The point is that *ad hoc* unilateral support for new towns of any sort by separate federal agencies (agriculture, HUD, and/or HEW, to name a few) creates policy by expedience. Rather, we should have a well thought-out set of policies and priorities, with an emphasis on strategic planning for implementation of this policy. Anthony Downs has brilliantly outlined five basic policy alternatives for the future of American cities.[36] These alternatives involve various combinations of the following sub-policy groupings:

A. Enrichment vs. Non-Enrichment

The choice here is between continuing present policies (minimal subsidization of the poor, programs under-funded, etc.) and creating programs designed to substantially improve the quality of life for the disadvantaged in our midst. Present programs would be vastly expanded — more jobs, a better welfare system, better housing and education would all ensue.[37]

B. Concentration vs. Dispersal (of minorities)

Here the choice is between continuing to concentrate (through racial prejudice or economic coercion) blacks and other ethnic minorities within the central cities and the alternative course of dispersing these groups throughout the urban region. (This choice is separate from, but related to, the question of segregation vs. integration, which follows).[38]

C. Segregation vs. Integration

Present policies effectively insure segregation of ethnic minorities, especially blacks. The alternative choice, of course, is integration.[39]

Based upon the five possible combinations of the above choices (Downs throws out the three others as being internally inconsistent — effective integration, for example, would be impossible without enrichment), Downs arrives at the following breakdown of policy alternatives:

1. Continuation of present policies (or non-policies): Non-enrichment, concentration, and segregation. This would ". . . provide relatively low-level welfare, educational, housing, job training, and other support to the most deprived groups in the population — both those who are incapable of working, such as the vast majority of public aid recipients, and those who might possibly work, but are unemployed because of their lack of skills, discrimination, lack of desire, or any other reason."[40] This non-enrichment would guarantee, when combined with the present degree of racial prejudice in the country, that the other two factors — concentration in the central city and segregation — would also continue.[41]

2. *Enrichment only:* Enrichment, concentration, and segregation. It would be possible to improve the quality of life in our central cities through massive injections of funds and programs designed to bring about such a result, without necessarily working toward dispersal or integration. The result would be better welfare, housing, education, and jobs in the inner city, where the level of opportunity would rise to rival the white suburbs.[42]

3. *Integrated core:* Enrichment, concentration, and integration (in the center only). Here the enrichment would be necessary to make the central cities attractive places to live for all. An up-grading in the quality of life for the concentrated minorities would permit a different environment to evolve, and would provide a situation into which whites would not mind moving. Thus, the central cities would become integrated while the suburbs would remain substantially lily-white.[43]

4. *Segregated dispersal:* Enrichment, dispersal, and segregation. Here the goal would be to enrich the underprivileged and to disperse "pockets" of minorities throughout the metropolitan area. (Downs did not go into this, but it would be possible to combine this alternative with the integrated core concept, thus creating an integrated core city and a dispersed minority population in "pockets" within the surrounding suburbs.) Enrichment would be necessary here, for otherwise a significant number of minority group members would not be able financially to make the move to the higher-income pockets. Segregation would remain in effect (either by design or by permitting present prejudices to remain in effect).[44]

5. The final alternative would be one calling for enrichment, dispersal, and integration — Integrated Dispersal. Here the lives of the disadvantaged would be enriched, enabling them to make more choices as to living conditions. Policies designed to encourage integration (in-migration of whites to the central cities and out-migration of blacks to the suburbs) would be put into effect. Further, these policies would be so designed as to discourage the formation of "pockets" in either locale. This would be brought about, if no other means were devised, through a quota system.[45]

Which alternative should be chosen? This, of course, is a matter of opinion which is somewhat beyond the scope of this book. However, a brief analysis of the probabilities involved in making the choice is in order.

Downs feels that the first alternative will be self-defeating, and that the result may well be social disorder which may:

... continue to spawn incidents, riots, and perhaps guerrilla warfare. Then existing local policy forces might have to be supplemented with para-military forces on continuous alert. Thus, the present-policies strategy might lead to further polarization of whites and Negroes and even to the creation of semi-martial law in big cities.[46]

The second alternative would lessen the probabilities of disorder and martial law by lessening the reasons for dissatisfaction which are present today. Nevertheless, it only negatively addresses the question of black-white polarization — a social question which may, in time, transcend the economic questions which would be met by the enrichment program.

There are strong arguments for the final three alternatives. It is likely that the order in which they are listed above is also the correct order as far as difficulty of implementation goes, although it may be that number four is as easy or easier than number three. However, alternatives three and four have inherent weaknesses which should be cautioned against. The integrated core idea may be what is needed to prevent the central cities from exploding, but it does not address the white suburbs in more than superficial terms. No matter how pleasant the city is made to live in, it is still likely that only a certain type of individual is likely to take advantage of the integrated core concept so much as to move back in from his haven in the suburbs. Furthermore, it is this person who is of the least concern as far as the black-white polarization is concerned. This alternative presupposes that the white suburbs will remain so, and this factor will in all liklihood produce suburban communities even less sympathetic to minorities and just as antagonistic to city-dwellers as suburbanites often are now.

Alternative four, on the other hand, presupposes something which may be even more dangerous. While the suburbs would be "integrated" by the inclusion of "pockets" of minority groups,

25

the central cities presumably will be enriched without integration and will tend to become more and more black. Thus, we will have the reverse of number 3, with a black city surrounded by integrated suburbs. Here one must wonder about the probable consequences this will have on the attitudes of blacks. There is the added danger that the "pockets" of dispersed blacks will become mini-ghettos, with enforced, rather than voluntary, constraints on movement. If this resulted, there would be little change from today, and the confrontation situation would be revived.

What is left is Downs' alternative 5 and the combination of alternatives 3 and 4. Either would avoid most of the problems listed above (except that the latter has the possible problem of the mini-ghetto), yet either would be very difficult to bring about.

Since each metropolitan area is different in total size, in the size of its ghetto, its economic base, its rate of growth, and even the rate of change of social attitudes, it would be essential for each metropolitan community to adopt its own strategy based on over-all national policy. Application of federal policy must be firm but flexible. The land assembly procedures set forth in this book could form a vital component of national urban policy. Along with housing, education, and employment, they could play a role in a total systems approach actually to solve urban problems, as opposed to merely talking about them and offering empty promises to the blacks and the poor.

If we are to achieve these objectives, three policy elements appear to be essential: (1) any workable land policy must have some built-in method for implementation; (2) it must be predicated on private initiative; and (3) it must be profitable for the private entrepreneur. Here I am referring to the kind of effective land planning that Western European countries have been able to achieve with their urban land policies. But we must do it within the context of the American free enterprise system. This is a big order. The questions are complex, as expressed in the introduction, and there are no simple solutions.

references/footnotes

[11] Jefferson said: "The mobs of great cities add just so much to the support of pure government, as sores do to the strength of the human body. It is the manners and spirit of a people which preserve a republic in vigour." White, Morton & Lucia, *The Intellectual Versus the City* (1964), pp. 25-26.

[12] Interview with Professor Paul Gates, Cornell University in Ithaca, New York, Oct. 16, 1967. See also Gates, *The Homestead Act: Free Land Policy in Operation*, 1862-1935, in Land Use Policy and Problems in the United States, p. 28 (Ottoson ed. 1963). Professor Gates pointed out that, though the railroads were responsible for the birth of many western towns and cities, with relatively few exceptions, they played little part in controlling their development.

[13] Clawson, *Land Use and Demand for Land in the United States*, in Modern Land Policy (1960), p.5. Wooten, Gertel and Pendleton, *Major Uses of Land and Water in the United States with Special Reference to Agriculture*, Agricultural Economic Report No. 13, Table 20 (1962).

[14] *Demographic Yearbook* (Publishing Service, UN, New York, N.Y., Sales No. 66 XIII I.)

[15] Pickard, *Dimension of Metropolitanism* (1967), p. 91.

[16] Kahn & Wiener. "A Framework for Speculation," *Daedalus* (Summer 1967), p. 719.

[17] Dickinson, "The Process of Urbanization," *Future Environments of North America* (Darling & Milton ed. 1966), p. 470.

[18] *Ibid.*

[19] Higbee, *The Squeeze* (1961), p. 3.

[20] Vernon, "The Changing Economic Function of the Central City," *Urban Renewal: The Record and the Controversy* (Wilson ed. 1966), p. 5.

[21] Vernon, *The Myth and Reality of Our Urban Problems* (1962), p. 32.

[22] Wingo, "The Use of Urban Land," *Land Use Policy and Problems in the United States* (Ottoson ed. 1963), p. 239.

[23] Whyte, "Urban Sprawl," *The Exploding Metropolis* (1958), pp. 115-40.

[24] Greer, *The Emerging City* (1962), p. 30.

[25] Whyte, "Urban Sprawl," *The Exploding Metropolis* (1958), p. 116.

[26] Perloff, "Modernizing Urban Development," *Daedalus* (Summer 1967), p. 793.

[27] Burroughs, "Should Urban Land be Publicly Owned?", *42 Land Economics* (1966), p. 11.

[28] Reich, "The New Property," *73 Yale Law Journal* (1964), p. 771.

[29] Burroughs, "Should Urban Land be Publicly Owned?", *42 Land Economics* (1966), p. 12.

[30] "Land: It's Still Housing's No. 1 Problem," *House and Home* (September 1964), p. 41.

[31] William L. Slayton, American Society of Planning Officials (ASPO) National Conference, Houston, Texas, March 1967.

[32] Remarks of Vice-President Hubert H. Humphrey before the "Communities of Tomorrow Conference," Washington, D.C., December 12, 1967.

[33] "Negroes to Build Their Own 'New Town' in North Carolina," *New York Times*, January 14, 1969, p. 43.

[34] Floyd B. McKissick, former head of the Congress of Racial Equality, *New York Times*, January 14, 1969, p. 43.

[35] Anthony Downs, "Alternative Futures for the American Ghetto," *Daedalus* (Fall 1968), p. 1338.

[36] *Ibid., pp. 1331-78.*

[37] *Ibid.*, p. 1344.

[38] *Ibid.*

[39] *Ibid.*

[40] *Ibid.*

[41] *Ibid.*, p. 1346.

[42] *Ibid.*, pp. 1346-47.

[43] *Ibid.*, pp. 1347-49.

[44] *Ibid.*, pp. 1349-51.

[45] *Ibid.*, pp. 1351-53.

[46] *Ibid.*, p. 1354.

Chapter 3

AN ANALYSIS:
URBAN RENEWAL AND NEW TOWNS

Our "urban problems" have been with us for many years. Like old friends, we know all their faults. There is even a danger that they might become comfortable old friends if the urban poor would only relax. In recent years we have even seen the phenomenon of environmental nihilism which denies that any valid values or standards exist — particularly regarding the quality of our urban environment. Exponents of this "new urban chaos" insist that there are rational explanations for the shape of urbanization. They claim that it contains valuable elements of vitality, variety, complexity and contrast. Architectural critic Ada Louise Huxtable calls this the "esthetic of pop landscape," the avant garde pop art of the 1960's and spread out across the land.

Architect Robert Venturi finds urban sprawl and the strip development of the superhighways, supermarkets, and supermotels an exhilerating esthetic experience and that this urban chaos contains its own order.[47] But, as critic Huxtable cautions, "There is always a dangerous tendency for reason and judgment to abdicate to fashionable ideas."[48] The problem with this simplistic line of reasoning is, of course, that fads change faster than the landscape and once it is polluted it must wait for urban renewal to become fashionable again. Meanwhile, it is an inefficient, uneconomic blight on the landscape. Such blighted landscapes become more critical as

29

the scope, magnitude and intensity of urban problems increase with the advent of the "urban crisis." In short, we must be quite clear that past efforts to find solutions to our problems have been a hit-and-miss proposition.

The two most significant concerns of spatial planning in America have been urban renewal and new towns. In other countries the two programs have been used together to eradicate slum dwelling and overcoming the relocation problem which has all but crippled renewal efforts here.

This brief analysis of the two programs is presented to provide the framework for a detailed discussion of the recommendations for land assembly. The urban renewal program has flourished and declined in twenty years. Enacted in 1949, it represents the first federal experience in assembling land to redevelop our central cities.[49] The "new town" concept is a more recent federal interest and it involves the assembly of land in suburban areas.

Urban Renewal and Rehabilitation

The urban renewal program has its roots in the slum clearance and housing projects initiated by the federal government back in the 1930's. In the early forties a few states, including New York and Illinois, passed legislation attempting to deal with the problems of urban growth and decay. New York enacted the Urban Redevelopment Corporation Act, and Illinois passed its Neighborhood Redevelopment Corporation Act.[50] These early efforts produced very limited results. Perhaps the most ambitious project under this legislation was Stuyvesant Town in New York City.

In 1941 the Federal Housing Administration published *A Handbook for Redevelopment in the United States,* which suggested the formation of city realty corporations with broad powers to acquire, hold and dispose of real property.[51] Later a more detailed proposal was advanced by Guy Greer and Alvin Hansen under the auspices of the National Planning Association.[52] These proposals were the basis for legislation which was introduced to Congress in 1943. Action on the proposed legislation was delayed by the Second World War, and also by controversial public housing provisions that were part of the same bill. It was not until 1949 that passage was achieved.

Title I of the Housing Act of 1949 provided for federal assistance to a local public agency for assembly, clearance, site preparation and sale or lease of land for urban renewal projects.[53] Local government was required to contribute an amount equal to one-third of the loss due to write-down of land prices. The federal government paid for the remaining two-thirds.[54] The 1954 amendments to the Act sought to place greater emphasis on rehabilitation and restoration of blighted areas, rather than total demolition and redevelopment. At the same time, other amendments were enacted adopting the requirement of a "workable program" intended to encourage the integration of urban renewal projects with plans for over-all community development.[55]

Since its inception, the primary thrust of the urban renewal program has been the elimination of slums. The original legislation had a provision which, in effect, limited urban renewal efforts to "better" housing. This was the "predominantly residential" provision which required that projects be initiated in deteriorating areas which already were, or were to be developed, predominantly for residential use.[56] Though the emphasis on housing was altered by the 1959 amendments, which allowed a substantial percentage of funds to go to non-residential projects, Congressional support has rested mainly on the elimination of blighted housing.[57]

Robert C. Weaver, former Secretary of HUD, declared, "The urban renewal program should be used in each locality to the full extent of its flexibilities and authorizations, and should not be limited to housing problems." He added, however, that housing is a significant objective of the program, and "It is inevitable that each local urban renewal program will establish its own practical and political priorities."[58] Though the debate on urban renewal priorities still continues, opinion is shifting toward the adoption of a more comprehensive program. "Urban renewal has evolved into a program whose concern with residential blight has led to concern with the whole of the urban physical environment."[59]

Urban renewal is oriented toward the central city. The primary emphasis is on blighted, slum areas of the core city rather than on regional development. However, the need for a broad metropolitan approach seems clear today.[60] Renewal efforts are hindered by the jurisdictional limits of the municipality.[61] One urban expert, Louis Winnick, program officer in charge of Urban and Metropolitan Redevelopment for the Ford Foundation, said:

> Public intervention in reshaping private land use is largely reserved for the city's weak areas . . . and is absent in strong areas where a considerable volume of private construction is taking place . . . Everywhere else the private developer is left virtually to his own devices, subject only to the limited and negative influence of building and zoning ordinances.[62]

Winnick goes on to say that the unaided private investor, no matter how enlightened, cannot give us a city in the image we desire. The emphasis should be changed from core area renewal to guiding the development of the entire urban region.

The Relocation Problem

Relocation is the biggest problem of the urban renewal program. Critics say the program has strong racial overtones, and many projects amount to Negro removal. Negroes removed from blighted areas are sometimes relocated in marginal areas which then deteriorate into slums.[63]

In Newark, New Jersey, for example, this problem became acute in 1958. Thirty-eight percent of the 800 families involved in the first project of the urban renewal program had to be relocated within the blighted area itself. The local housing authority was forced to house an additional twenty-three percent of these families in marginal areas surrounding the ghetto. This brought harsh reactions from both Negro and white communities. Complaints were made that the program tended to increase overcrowding in the ghetto and caused the spread of blighted areas.[64]

Public housing provides a partial answer to the problems of finding adequate quarters for relocated families. Many families, however, are unwilling or unable to move into such housing. Either they do not qualify for housing assistance, or they refuse such assistance because of a basic prejudice against subsidized housing.[65]

Another aspect of the relocation problem is the financial and goodwill losses suffered by neighborhood businesses. In Newark, approximately forty percent of the businesses displaced by renewal projects discontinued their operations. The survival rate is lowest for small businesses where low rent and a personal relationship with the clientele are valuable assets.[66] Compared to some other nations, urban renewal seems to offer inadequate compensation for commercial dislocation. Though payments are made for commercial relocation, those who are not able to continue in business feel they have been deprived of their livelihood and should be compensated accordingly. Even businesses able to continue operations claim they have suffered substantial uncompensated losses.[67]

In Holland and Belgium, all the costs of relocating a business are figured into a total "package deal" which appears to be more reasonable. There, compensation includes (1) "disturbance" costs, (2) reinvestment costs, and (3) interest charges.[68] This solution seems to provide a more desirable basis for a compensation formula.

Local Costs of the Program

Local governments face an acute problem in financing their share of an urban renewal program. Though it is claimed that these projects add tax revenue to a city's income, municipalities are unable to meet their fiscal obligations from property tax receipts.[69] It has been contended that increases in tax receipts due to urban renewal projects are not as substantial as local governments have been led to believe.[70] The city is allowed to pay for part of its share by non-cash grants. This provision, however, tends to encourage municipal officials to select renewal areas where public works are already being planned. Such projects are then used as part of the city's contribution. Conversely, it also causes municipalities to defer expenditures for needed parks, playgrounds and schools until an urban renewal project including these facilities is approved.[71]

The necessity of meeting local contribution requirements also causes other problems. City officials tend to view renewal projects as real estate transactions. They are interested in getting the highest price possible for the land in order to reduce the cost of the project. This programmatic orientation "is not conducive to the achievement of much broader design and social objectives."[72] In addition, the city has been promised increased tax revenues to meet project costs. This encourages the city to approve projects for luxury housing, such as Kips Bay in New York, which will allow the project to pay for itself.[73] The mayors of our major American cities are calling for a reduction in the local share of project costs. Perhaps the desirability of *any* local participation should be questioned.

Finding a Developer

One federal official claimed that private redevelopers are ready and willing to bid for urban renewal land, and cited William Zeckendorff and Alcoa as prominent examples.[74] Zeckendorff, however, has since suffered financial reverses, and Leon E. Hickman of Alcoa once noted, "There is plainly something wrong" when, by mid-1963, cities had acquired 21,970 acres and renewal was completed or in process on only 6,130 acres. Hickman went on to say that while it was true that developers had been selected for fifty-eight percent of the acquired acreage, selection of a developer does not mean he will ever buy or build on the land.[75]

The contention that developers are readily available is disputed by other renewal experts. Charles Abrams says bidding for urban renewal sites is "unspirited" and that many cities have a great deal of difficulty interesting a developer in their projects. The city of New Brunswick, New Jersey, spent years searching for a developer for its downtown projects.[76]

James Appel, Vice-President of Roy Wenzlick & Company, pointed out that a survey taken by his company disclosed many urban renewal sites available, but with no takers. "This is an embarrassment to the entire program, and greater emphasis is now being taken to secure competent land utilization and marketability studies before freezing plans which might prove unsuitable."[77]

The situation is changing. More developers are becoming interested in renewal projects. But we must conclude that for many communities finding a developer is still a tough problem.

Land utilization and marketability studies may help. The problem will be resolved, however, only by closer cooperation with the private developer prior to project initiation.

A Look at Rehabilitation

Emphasis on rehabilitation of existing neighborhoods and structures, rather than demolition, began with the 1954 revisions to the Housing Act. It was part of the growing reaction against wholesale slum clearance projects. Rehabilitation was advanced as an answer to the problem of social dislocation caused by outright clearance and rebuilding.[78] Presumably, rehabilitation involves only temporary relocation for inhabitants of the project area.

The record shows, however, that this acclaim has not been unanimous. Rehabilitation has not eliminated the problem of dislocation. "Rehab" critics point out that relocated persons prefer to make a single permanent move. Moreover, it has not provided cheaper housing for low income groups. There are too many instances where rehabilitation has cost more than constructing new housing.[79]

Others point our that, although rehabilitation has been tried successfully, these experiments were on a very modest scale. It is argued that, if such a program were substantially expanded, private funds would not be available. Supposedly, banks would refuse to loan money for rehabilitation because of blighted conditions in surrounding neighborhoods and the difficulty of obtaining insurance. On the other hand, Martin Anderson contends that if public funds are to be used it would have to be on a massive scale, and in conjunction with rent control legislation.[80]

The sad fact is that we have more rehab studies than projects. One recent study has indicated that selective rehabilitation can provide better housing, at a reasonable price, and without the necessity of substantial increases in rent.[81] Another study of rehabilitation in Baltimore, Chicago, Miami and New Orleans shows that rehabilitation can improve neighborhood attitudes. The people involved seem to feel it leads to a better way of life.[82]

If a rehabilitation program is planned as an integral part of an urban renewal project that also includes clearance and

35

rebuilding, it can play a vital role.[83] Rehabilitation should be part of any federal housing program, but it will never be the primary or exclusive answer to the slum housing problem. If a city is going to undertake large-scale rehabilitation, it must also offer an attractive place to live. Only in this way can the rehab process be made effective.[84] The Model Cities program attempts to achieve these coordinated objectives.

According to an August, 1967, HUD evaluation of rehabilitation programs under Section 110(c) of the Housing Act of 1949, the following factors "limit massive rehabilitation": (a) The difficult and complex nature of property rehabilitation, where each individual situation involves its own peculiar combination of "owner motivation, physical and financial characteristics of the property and environmental factors;" (b) the lack of "legislative support for rehabilitation activities at the city level;" (c) the shortage of "trained staff, adequate in numbers and skills to provide effective service to property owners;" (d) the need for cities to "increase the number and size of rehabilitation projects in order to develop a better balance between rehabilitation and clearance;" (e) the need for "more effective molding of urban renewal and anti-poverty programs at the local level;" and (f) the need for "cities to make firm commitments to provide the public improvements and neighborhood services needed in rehabilitation areas if deterioration is to be arrested and the values of property improvements are to be sustained."[85] The HUD evaluation is largely an indictment of the ability of local government to deal with the complexities of rehabilitation. The evaluation is fair, however. An effective rehabilitation program must rely on local initiative.

Urban Renewal and Rehabilitation in Summary

In his book, *The Federal Bulldozer,* Martin Anderson complained that the urban renewal program has been a failure, and that its objectives can be gained only by the free enterprise system. Such criticism is neither justified nor realistic. While it is true that urban renewal has had difficulty in achieving its goals, it has also scored many brilliant successes, especially in downtown commercial redevelopment. Rehabilitation has great potential, but is limited by the lack of local initiative. The question is, where should urban renewal go in the future? It seems clear that we need (1) greater participation by the private developer in the selection of renewal projects, and (2) a regional approach to urban renewal.

The New Towns Concept

The American approach to new town development is one of the least understood and most widely abused concepts on the American urban scene. Planners say, "New approaches to the settlement of urban areas are desperately needed, and new towns offer one of the soundest of these approaches."[86] The concept of new towns is indeed intriguing. It also has political appeal. For instance, Senator Edward M. Kennedy called on America's homebuilders to "help rebuild the nation's slum areas and establish new towns on the fringes of the cities' suburbs to meet the problems of massive population growth."[87]

Former President Eisenhower, quoted in an editorial in the New York Times on April 29, 1968, suggested that relocation in "new, more wholesome communities" is "the first essential" in any realistic plan to eliminate city slums. Federal financial support is imperative, he noted, although "the impetus, the planning and the doing must be at the community level."

For those who hope to redevelop our deteriorating urban cores, new towns offer an opportunity to provide relocation housing. Others visualize rings of new communities, linked to the central city by high-speed transit systems as a solution to "spread city" with its characteristic "creeping sprawl." The new town philosophy also appeals to those who believe today's cities are beyond saving, and that we should start all over again with new cities in the clean countryside.

In January 1969, 200 urban planners from thirteen eastern states gathered at a meeting euphemistically called "Conference 2020" to discuss the physical shape of the Atlantic region today, to consider how that arrangement affects people, and to plot the region's desired form half a century from now.

In a poll conducted at the conference by Elmo Roper, 70 percent of the conferees said they wanted some form of suburban and exurban concentrations — outlying mini-cities, as it were, tied to

37

each other and to the central core by appropriate new transportation systems — to be the goal of urban development for the next half-century.[88]

The new town concept is deceptively simple. Many of the more complicated problems such as financing, governmental friction, social resistance, and transportation, are familiar only to the handful who have tried to build new towns. A workable new towns program could play a significant part in the future growth of our urban America, but such problems must be dealt with realistically if new towns are to realize their full potential.

Most definitions of new towns are vague and confusing. Generally, however, new towns fall into two broad categories: (1) satellite communities, and (2) self-contained new towns. Satellite communities may provide for commercial and even some industrial land uses, but they are essentially dependent on an existing city. The basic function of a satellite is to provide housing for metropolitan "spillover." The Scandinavian new towns are more characteristic of this type. The second classification, the self-contained new town, is designed to provide a balanced residential, commercial and industrial environment. Dependence on adjacent cities is discouraged. The classic English garden city model is separated from other communities by a permanent "green belt."

New towns should not be confused with the common garden variety "bedroom" community. The new towns concept calls for a balanced environment for living, working and playing, within an attractive and efficient physical framework. The "one-class, one-color, uniform bedroom community" does not fit this idea.

The British New Towns

Ebenezer Howard's enthusiasm and zeal was the driving force behind the original British "new town." Howard initiated a private company in 1903 to begin the construction of Letchworth, the first "garden city." It was designed as a self-contained community, with its own shops and factories, on a rural site about 40 miles from London. The company retained the freehold and leased individual building sites, thus permitting control over individual design and development. The growth of Letchworth, however, was quite slow. The site was unattractive, completely undeveloped, and too distant from downtown London. In addition, the original land costs were high, and heavy interest charges on ensuing mortgages created financial difficulties for the company. It was forty-three years before all accumulated dividends were repaid to investors.[89] Front money, or "bridging finance" as the British call it today, is still a most critical problem in building new towns.

The second new town, Welwyn Garden City (1920), was also beset with financial problems growing out of undercapitalization. Welwyn differed from Letchworth in that the development company intended to reserve for itself a virtual monopoly in the operation of many profitable enterprises. These included, at various times, the electrical and building companies, a theatre, gravel plant, brickworks and a railway.[90] In addition, the company itself built many of the commercial and industrial facilities, which were then let out on short-term leases. This policy served a dual function. First, it made it possible for new enterprises to begin operations with small capital outlays. Second, it gave the development company the benefits of increasing property values, for new rents were negotiated at the end of each lease period.

Toward the end of World War II, the British government undertook a program for the reconstruction of London and other war-torn cities. Sir Patrick Abercrombie's Greater London Plan (1944), proposed the establishment of a series of satellite towns in a ring some 20 miles from the downtown center. The Reith Committee was appointed to consider the feasibility of a national "new towns" policy, and favorable reports were presented.[91] These resulted in the New Towns Act, passed by Parliament on August 1, 1946.

The Act provided for the designation of new town sites by the Minister of Town and Country Planning, who was also empowered to establish development corporations to plan and build the new towns. These corporations have the power to acquire land compulsorily, to "hold, manage and dispose of land and other property, to carry on any business or undertaking in or for the purposes of the new town, and generally to do anything necessary or expedient for the purposes of the new town or for purposes incidental thereto." To date, some 21 new towns have been established, ranging in population from 2,500 to 67,800.

On balance, the British new town experience has been successful. The residents from overcrowded neighborhoods in large cities have gained clean air and open space. They moved into modern homes with gardens, convenient to schools, churches and places of work.[92] However, the attracting of white-collar industries to the new towns has remained a major problem.

The Swedish New Towns

Scandinavian new towns have differed significantly from those in Britain, where the program is administered at the national level. The British philosophy is to limit central city growth, and to encourage the development of completely new self-contained communities. Green belts ring the new towns, supposedly discouraging commuting to the central city or other new towns because of the distances involved.

Swedish new towns, on the other hand, tend to follow the satellite pattern, and usually are dependent on an established city. The U.S. new towns, such as Reston and Columbia, are closer to the Swedish model.

The city of Stockholm planned for future growth by initiating a land purchase program over sixty years ago. Over 50,000 acres were acquired, and this land has been used to house Stockholm's growing population as the need arose. On it have been built efficient and attractive new towns, such as Vallingby and Farsta. These communities, essentially residential, are linked to the central city by clean, well-lighted commuter train systems.

Finnish New Towns

A comparison of Finnish new towns with those of other countries demonstrates that good design cannot be legislated. The Finns, with an absence of governmental land-use controls, have achieved a very high level of design. Others do not equal this, despite their ostensibly more extensive "control" over esthetic design considerations. (Of course, this may be more a reflection on various nationality characteristics than a commentary on the effectiveness of land-use and design controls.) New towns, such as Tapiola (which is largely completed) and Esspo (still in the early planning stages), are among the finest new communities to be found anywhere in the world, particularly in terms of site planning, landscape design, and architectural sensitivity. Finland demonstrates that a system based on private enterprise can produce, with a slight assist from government, attractive and well-designed satellite communities.

New Towns in the United States

There are no self-contained new towns in the United States. The Housing and Home Finance Agency (the predecessor of HUD) once estimated that there are presently more than 100 "new communities" or "satellite cities" under construction. Upon examination, however, most of these prove to be little more than variations on the "bedroom community" theme. Outstanding exceptions are Columbia, Maryland, and Irvine, California.

As William L. C. Wheaton has said,

"The United States alone among the major nations of the world has failed to adopt and implement some sort of new towns policy. We particularly need planned new cities to set design standards for a population which has come to accept scattered, unorganized growth as the norm. We have few distinguished examples of how beautiful an urban area can be."[93]

Planned community development is not a new concept in the United States. Radburn, New Jersey, and the "Greenbelt Towns" of the 1930's in Maryland, Ohio and Wisconsin, represent early attempts to impose comprehensive land planning on the design of entire communities. These early efforts were useful attempts to advance the art by providing a totally planned new environment. They were not, however, new towns in the British sense.

More than a dozen new large-scale suburban developments, or communities, are completed or well under way in California. The old Spanish land grants provide large tracts of preassembled land readily available for new town development.

One of the largest is on the 90,000-acre Irvine Ranch in Orange County, which was designed to create a total urban complex for an ultimate population of 100,000. The plan provides for a commercial center, ample industrial acreage, and a new University of California campus. Laguna Niguel at South Laguna and the 80,000-acre proposed development at San Simeon, south of Monterey, are two more examples.

American industry has begun to take the initiative in new community planning. Kaiser Industries is involved in the proposed 87,500-acre Vail Ranch project near Los Angeles. Goodyear, Humble Oil and Standard Oil of New Jersey have new towns under way or in the planning stage. Alcoa and General Electric have also expressed an interest in the development of new towns.

The original plan for Reston, Virginia, represents one of our best examples of new town planning. Reston is a 6,800-acre project designed for a population of 75,000. A residential "high density sinew" winds through the tract putting recreation areas within walking distance for all. Town houses and garden apartments comprise 70 percent of the residential community. Open space has been given special attention at Reston, where "each acre has a purpose; if it is open, it is not by default but by plan."[94]

Columbia, Maryland, located between Washington and Baltimore, may well become the most successful of the new towns now under way in the United States. Like Reston, the physical plan was designed to emphasize social function. In an attempt "to acknowledge learning as a basic foundation for a human community,"[95] schools will be the focal point for each level of community life. Each neighborhood and village complex will contain schools, parks, playgrounds, a swimming pool, shopping facilities and "meeting" or community rooms. A "mini-bus" service will eliminate the need for a second car. The downtown cultural center will provide theatres, art galleries and studios.

Problems of New Town Development

New town developers face many complex problems, but the two biggest are land and money. From Letchworth to Reston, new communities have typically been too far away to suit the housing market. Poor location is usually attributable to the developers' inability to assemble large quantities of land, in the right location, at reasonable prices.

Financing a new town is a complex and difficult matter. It took 43 years to "finance" Letchworth. The problem of raising working capital has separated the talkers from the builders. New town developers trying to go it alone have run into financial difficulties. Robert Simon, Jr., was recently forced to turn over control of Reston to his largest backer, Gulf Oil Corporation.

President Johnson's early attempts to provide federal aid for new towns ran into heavy congressional opposition. The Administration supported the 1966 Urban Redevelopment Act which provided aid for new communities as an essential element of a balanced program for regional development. It also encouraged small developers to participate in new town construction. This measure was designed to gain broader political support among builders and the National Association of Home Builders of the U.S.

New towns need industry for several reasons.. Industry broadens their tax base. It minimizes commuter travel. It attracts residents to new towns. A Newsweek report on Reston's misfortunes said, "Most of Reston's residents are very happy there — but there just aren't enough of them."[96] Long distance commuting and the lack of local employment opportunities were responsible.

On balance, new towns have tremendous potential. However, efficient land assembly techniques and procedures must be provided if the development of new communities is to meet the problems of urban America in providing the six million new housing units for low and middle-income families called for in the next ten years.

---

[47] "The Case for Chaos," *New York Times*, January 26, 1969, p. 32.

[48] *Ibid.*

[49] Title I, Housing Act of 1949, 63 Stat. 413, 42 U.S.C. § 441 (1949).

references/footnotes

[50] By 1949, 23 states and the District of Columbia had some type of redevelopment legislation; by 1958 all but 8 states had legislation or constitutional provisions which authorized local public agencies to undertake renewal efforts. See Sogg and Werthheimer, "Legal and Governmental Issues in Urban Renewal," in *Urban Renewal: The Record and the Controversy* (Wilson ed. 1966), p. 130.

[51] Foard and Fefferman, "Federal Urban Renewal Legislation," in *Urban Renewal: The Record and the Controversy* (Wilson ed. 1966), pp. 71-72.

[52] *Ibid.*, p. 73. This is not an implication that the Greer-Hansen proposal was based on the FHA Handbook.

[53] Title I Housing Act of 1949, 63 Stat. 413, 43 U.S.C. § 441 (1949).

[54] See §§ 103 (a), 104, 106 (f), 110 (d), (e), (f) of the Housing Act of 1949.

[55] See Abrams, *The City is the Frontier* (1965), p. 87. The author views the 1954 amendments as the turning point in the history of the urban renewal program. See also, D.C. Office of Urban Renewal, *Review of Progress Under a Workable Program for Community Improvement* (1964), which was submitted to the FHA. The report includes sections on code enforcement, community planning, housing, financing, administrative organizations, etc.

[56] Foard and Fefferman, "Federal Urban Renewal Legislation," in *Urban Renewal: The Record and the Controversy* (Wilson ed. 1966) p. 104.

[57] Housing Act of 1959, 73 Stat. 672, 42 U.S.C.A. §1453 (1959). The Housing Act of 1959 and later amendments have broadened the scope of urban renewal and allowed a significant percentage of federal assistance to be used for non-residential development.

[58] Lowe, *Urban Renewal Influx* (1966), p. 67.

[59] Slayton, "New Concepts of the Business Community & Urban Renewal," in *Institute for Community Development & Services, Urban Renewal and Private Enterprise* (1962), p. 36.

[60] See Charles M. Haar, "Regionalism and Realism in Land Use Planning," 105 U. Pa. Law Review (1957), p. 515.

[61] "Unless the use of land in a particular project area is planned with as full a knowledge and understanding of the changing land use patterns of the entire metropolitan community, the probability is great that the redeveloped area is already on its way toward another round of blight and obsolescence." Jones, "Local Government Organization in Metropolitan Areas," in *Future of the Cities and Urban Development* (Woodbury ed. 1953), p. 604.

[62] Winnick, "Facts and Fictions in Urban Renewal," in *Urban Housing* (Wheaton ed. 1966), pp. 441-42.

[63] Anderson, *The Federal Bulldozer* (1964), p. 8.

[64] Kaplan, *Urban Renewal Politics* (1963), p. 157.

[65] Dean, "The Myth of Housing Reform," in *Urban Housing* (Wheaton ed. 1966), pp. 255-57.

[66] Zimmer, "The Small Business and Relocation," in *Urban Renewal: The Record and the Controversy* (Wilson ed. 1966), p. 382.

[67] *Ibid.* at 391.

[68] These compensation procedures are explained in detail in the Foreign Experience Section.

[69] Dyckman, *Capital Requirements for Urban Development and Renewal* (1961), pp. 7-8.

[70] Anderson, *The Federal Bulldozer* (1964), p. 162.

[71] Sogg & Werthheimer, "Legal and Governmental Issues in Urban Renewal," in *Urban Renewal: The Record and the Controversy* (Wilson ed. 1966), p. 136.

[72] Slayton, "Implementation: Urban Renewal," in *The Regional City* (Senior ed. 1966), p. 95.

[73] Lowe, *Urban Renewal in Flux* (1966), pp. 20-21.

[74] McFarland, "Urban Renewal," in *Urban Housing* (Wheaton ed. 1966), p. 436.

[75] Kay, "The Third Force in Urban Renewal," in *Fortune* (October 1964), pp. 130-33.

[76] Abrams, *The City is the Frontier* (1965), pp. 98-99.

[77] Appel, "What Has Been the Private Investment Experience in Urban Renewal?", *Urban Renewal in Private Enterprise* (Institute for Community Development and Services, 1962), p. 42.

[78] Abrams, *The City is the Frontier* (1965), p. 185. The author notes the great emphasis placed on rehabilitation and conservation by the late President Kennedy in 1961.

[79] Lowe, *Urban Renewal in Flux* (1966), pp. 40-45: "The supposed virtues of rehabilitation . . . were two-fold . . . it eliminated need to dislocate families, and . . . it allowed them to live in houses they can afford. Actually, neither result is achieved in most instances."

[80] Anderson, *The Federal Bulldozer* (1964), pp. 157-59.

[81] Johnson, "The Quality of Housing Before and After Rehabilitation," in *Urban Housing* (Wheaton ed. 1966), p. 408.

[82] As one teen-ager commented, "This used to be a crummy neighborhood, but now it's all fixed up." Millspaugh, *The Lessons Learned in Urban Housing* (1966), p. 481.

[83] Dyckman, *Captial Requirements for Urban Development and Renewal* (1961), p. 74.

[84] Abrams, *The City is the Frontier*, (1965), p. 187.

[85] *Rehabilitation Programs:* A Committee Print prepared by the Dept. of Housing & Urban Development for the Subcommittee on Housing & Urban Affairs of the Committee on Banking & Currency; United States Senate, 90th Congress, 1st Session, August 1967. Govt. Printing Office, Washington, 1967.

[86] Gladstone & Wise, "New Towns Solve Problems of Urban Growth," *New Towns* (International City Manager's Association 1966), p. 22.

45

[87] *New York Times.* December 5, 1967. Senator Kennedy's address before the National Association of Home Builders, Chicago, Illinois, December 5, 1967.

[88] William K. Stevens, "Urban Planners Focus on Reality," *New York Times,* February 2, 1969.

[89] Rodwin, *The British New Towns Policy* (1956), p. 13.

[90] Osborn and Whittick, *The New Towns* (1963), p. 49.

[91] H. M. Stationery Office (1946), Cmd. 6759, 6794, 6876.

[92] Kirk, "New Towns in Great Britain," in *New Towns* (International City Manager's Association 1966), p. 11.

[93] William L.C. Wheaton, address before the 1966 Conference of the American Institute of Planners, Portland, Oregon, August, 1966.

[94] Simon, "Planning a New Town - Reston, Virginia," *Planning 1964,* p. 153.

[95] Bailey, "Only in Columbia, The Next America," *The Architectural Forum* (Nov. 1967), p. 44.

[96] *Newsweek,* Nov. 22, 1967.

Chapter 4

LAND ASSEMBLY: THE FOREIGN EXPERIENCE

In the United States, the public role in urbanization and land development has been essentially negative. Local planning agencies are overwhelmingly concerned with the administration of negative land use controls such as zoning and subdivision controls. The lessons to be drawn from the experience of England, Holland, Belgium and the Scandinavian countries, however, are largely positive ones. There land is regarded as a resource rather than a commodity. The lessons of each country are different, but the public philosophy — the urban land policy — is constant. The quality of life is intricately tied to the quality of the environment, and public land purchase is a vital part of effective public planning. National, regional and municipal agencies have established programs for buying land and then selling or leasing it for development in accord with community plan. The success of Stockholm's planning, the elimination of slums and quality of suburban growth, can be attributed directly to the Swedish public land purchase program. In contrast, however, it should be noted that land for the brilliantly successful Finnish new town, Tapiola, was assembled by private funds. Land can be assembled, but it is becoming more and more difficult in an increasingly urbanized world.

A wide variety of land assembly techniques and procedures are found in other countries. Land development is often initiated at the national level in England, the municipal level in Sweden, and by a combination of private and public enterprise in Finland. Yet all three have provided land for well-planned new communities. In England and Holland, land acquired by government agencies is usually sold for private development purposes, although leasing or governmental development is possible. The city of Stockholm, on the other hand, has been buying and "banking" land both in and around the city for 60 years. This land is then leased to private interests.

Compulsory purchase, the common European term for condemnation, is practiced under widely varying circumstances. Belgium and England have "quick take" procedures under which possession can be taken within approximately six months. In the Netherlands and Belgium, compulsory purchase legislation requires generous compensation. As a result, expropriation is more acceptable, and voluntary compromise is commonplace in land acquisition proceedings. Finland has never had compulsory purchase legislation, although the administration now feels condemnation powers are necessary and a new program will soon be put before the legislature.

The new British Land Commission is designed to encourage private and local land development, while providing a measure of national control over major policies and programs. These policies and programs should provide a working model of methods and techniques which could, at least in part, be utilized in the United States.

ENGLAND

England's modern land use planning system began with the Town and Country Planning Act of 1947. Under this Act, strong powers to plan and control land use were delegated to some 150 county and borough councils, each of which was responsible for the preparation of a 20-year development plan for its area. These plans were submitted to the Minister of Housing and Local Government for review at the national level, and usually underwent substantial modification before being approved. In England the Minister is the supreme land use planning authority and is endowed with a broad range of regulatory and initiative planning powers. In practice, however, the exercise of these powers and the implementation of plans has been difficult, and the results mixed. As a consequence, proposed modifications of certain procedures in the Town and Country Planning Act were expected to become law in 1968.

Local planning authorities use town and county plans to guide land development. Planning permission is needed to change, renew or in any way modify existing uses of land. According to the law, local plans are reviewed every five years to insure their conformance with changing times and needs, and must be resubmitted to the Minister for approval.

England has long followed the philosophy that the public, as well as individual owners, should reap profits due to increases in land values brought about by public improvements and planning controls. Various methods for taxing this increase, called "betterment," were incorporated into the Planning Acts of 1925 and 1932. A new and sweeping form of development charges was provided in the revised Town and Country Planning legislation of 1947, but under this Act the collection of betterment levies was, for the most part, a failure. Individual property owners were reluctant to sell or develop their land due to the imposition of the "betterment levy," and frequently attempted to "pass on" the tax to the purchaser. The system proved to be unworkable.[97]

Town and Country Planning legislation has also offered various provisions dealing with the compulsory purchase of land. Under the 1947 Act local authorities could designate land to be acquired compulsorily, but at the national level this power was rather closely restricted. For this reason, and also due to the negative impact of the betterment tax, the 1947 Act provided for a Central Land Board which was given power to acquire land by eminent domain and dispose of it on the open market. This policy, however, was met with both public and judicial criticism, and the Board was not able to achieve the goals set for it.

The development charge was abandoned in 1954. By this time, post-war restrictions on building had been lifted, the economy was booming, and pressure for more private, speculative development increased. Beginning in 1959 the Government de-emphasized acquisition by condemnation, and land was purchased at the open market value.

The resultant increases in land costs and the re-establishment of the socialist government led up to England's newest land use control agency, the Land Commission.[98] The following section will analyze the new Land Commission as it relates to this study's recommendations for land assembly methods and techniques in the United States. For this reason only passing attention will be given the second major responsibility of the Commission, which is the collection of a betterment tax equal to 40 percent of the development value realized on the sale or development of land.[99] This, in effect, acts as a capital gains tax on the increase in development value, except that such gain will be realized when an owner redevelops his property as well as when it is sold.

The Land Commission

Over the past two decades, the problem of local initiative became increasingly difficult under existing Town and Country Planning legislation, due primarily to inadequate financing, opposition by property owners, and political inertia. Accordingly, pressure developed to set up a Land Commission designed to formulate workable land policies and programs at the national level. This resulted in a Land Commission Bill, proposed in 1965, which went into effect in September, 1967. The Commission is responsible for carrying out a government land policy, with its two main objectives being (1) to secure the right land at the right time for implementation of national, regional and local plans, and (2) to retain for the public a substantial portion of the increase in land values due to community development.[100]

Organization

The Land Commission is composed of a chairman and not more than eight other members, appointed jointly by the Minister of Land and Natural Resources and the Secretary of State for Scotland.[101] The present Commission membership represents balanced interests. It includes a private developer, realtor, home builders, politician, a lawyer and financier.[102] The Chairman is Sir Henry Wells, past President of The Royal Institute of Chartered Surveyors, real estate consultant, Chairman of the Commission for New Towns, and generally acknowledged as designer and chief advocate of the Land Commission. The Commission has 13 regional offices in Britain, including one in Scotland and one in Wales. Each regional office is divided into two divisions: A land division, and another for the collection of betterment levies. In the fall of 1967 these offices were operating with a "limited staff" of some 1200. A staff of 2000 is authorized, but for reasons of economy, it will probably be kept at 1200.[103]

Functions

The Land Commission will function as "a national land dealing corporation," according to Sir Henry. It is charged with "a very positive role which, briefly stated, is to ensure that private developers, large and small, and public authorities, including, of course, local authorities, get the land they require for their needs."[104] Sir Henry has frequently stressed the encouragement of private development as the fundamental means by which plan implementation will be achieved. "Too often the public and the private sectors seem not so much to be mixing as to be in a state of confrontation. I believe the Land Commission . . . can become a partner of the private sector."[105]

While physical development itself will be provided by private enterprise, there has been no hesitation to relegate the decision-making process to central government. "We must assume," said Sir Henry, "that the central government is the only body able to make the necessary judgments in the light of all the pressures — regional, economic, social — yes, and political, if one is being realistic"[106]

Mechanics of Land Acquisition

The Land Commission has wide powers of land acquisition. It may purchase by agreement any land thought to be needed for development, and, in addition, may effect compulsory purchase subject to several broadly-defined conditions. These powers may not be invoked until there has been a "planning decision" that the land is suitable for "material development,"[107] but beyond that, specific limitations will rely primarily on the discretion of the Land Commission itself.[108]

Compulsory purchase procedures have been streamlined and simplified. They are initiated with the filing of a compulsory purchase order by the Commission. If the landowner objects, it is necessary only to seek confirmation of the order from a Minister.[109] Once the order has been confirmed, the Commission can make a "general vesting declaration" which passes good title immediately, and possession can be taken after 28 days.[110] The settlement of compensation is an independent proceeding, and usually takes place at some later date.[111]

Management and Disposal of Land

In the normal course of events the Commission will hold land for the shortest period possible. However, the Commission is empowered to hold, manage and develop land when desirable.[112] The disposal policy is designed to be flexible and will usually take the form of either an outright sale or a very long term lease.[113]

The flexibility of the entire land program is aptly demonstrated by a hypothetical situation devised by Sir Henry Wells. Assume that a builder has negotiated unsuccessfully for a particular piece of land ripe for development, and has offered a fair price. The owner is unwilling to sell. If the Commission is satisfied that the proposed development is desirable, it can acquire the land compulsorily and pass title directly to the builder, without inviting others to compete.[114]

Sir Henry envisions the Land Commission as playing a commanding role in the assembly of land for private developers. "I believe," he said, "that it will be found convenient, by private developers, and by many local authorities, to rely on the Land Commission for acquiring and assembling the land needed for schemes of comprehensive development."[115]

The Land Commission Act of 1967 allocated up to 70 million pounds for land expropriation, although limited to six million pounds per year. The Land Commission expects to achieve fiscal independence, in time, by building up a "revolving" fund through land sales. The procedure is as follows: (1) the treasury provides seed money; (2) the money is invested in land; (3) after realization of betterment there is a regular payment to the treasury; and (4) the revolving funds can then be used for more land purchases.

The Role of the Private Developer

According to Professor Nathaniel Lichfield,[116] who has served as economic consultant for several new town developments, every new town is initiated and developed as a special case, with each town having its own Development Corporation. But there is a standard procedure for both land expropriation and new town development in the United Kingdom, and each Corporation acts individually under the central control of the Ministry of Housing and Local Government. Private developers are encouraged to participate in all forms of land use (housing, industrial and commericial), usually on land leased to them by the Corporation. Whereas the earlier new towns offered predominantly public housing (provided by the Corporation and local authority), the more recent trend is toward more private housing, with a 50/50 split being the ultimate objective. There have also been attempts to build new towns soley by private enterprise. In this situation the Land Commission is expected to be extremely useful in the assembly of needed lands.[117]

The British Land Commission in Summary

The Land Commission is a cooperative effort since it is dependent on planning by local government, but is also a device to assist the private developer. The key objective, according to Land Commission member Wyndham Thomas, is to "get moving on land which has been allocated for urbanization but has not yet been used."[118]

Because of speculation on land which has been allocated for development, but not used, the land becomes sterilized. The expropriation of these lands will release them for development in accordance with local land use plans. The Ministry of Housing has determined that there is enough land available, within the framework of existing plans, for 20 years of urbanization. But the problem is that local government will not take the initiative. The effect of this is economic sterilization of the land. The role of the Land Commission in this situation will be to act as a guarantor for the purchase of land by local governments.

The Land Commission will also pursue the policy of assembling land presently held in scattered ownership and therefore not available for large-scale development. The Commission will acquire such land and hold it for the future, on the theory that advance acquisition will be more economical in the long run.

NORWAY

The assembly of land for housing projects, new communities and public works projects has traditionally been a complicated and time-consuming process in Norway. Most land around cities is divided into very small, privately-owned parcels. To deal with this problem, the Ministry of Municipal Affairs and Labor has organized an ad hoc committee to speed-up expropriation procedures and streamline land assembly techniques. At present, expropriation normally requires two years, and three to four-year delays are not uncommon.

Problems of land assembly have been mitigated to some extent by widespread land lease practices. Both privately and publicly-owned lands are made available for private development under long term leases. Municipalities in particular have made extensive use of this practice since the middle 1950's. There are two factors which stimulate leasing rather than the outright sale of privately-owned property in Norway. National land-price controls have been in effect since World War II. Generally, inflation runs well ahead of the price structure established by these regulations. Thus the sale of land would involve a loss for many owners. In addition, a high tax rate on all profits derived from land sales increases the advantages of long-term leasing.

In 1946, Norway enacted two major pieces of legislation dealing with expropriation. The Expropriation Act, aimed at securing land for housing and future municipal building needs, included provisions which permitted the use of eminent domain procedures by social or cooperative building societies, and by private builders under certain conditions.

Under the Reconstruction Act whole areas were expropriated and replanned by municipalities. Original owners were assigned new sites as compensation for properties taken. This Act applied only to war-damaged districts, and is unused today. However, the technique could be applied in any area where total redevelopment is necessary. It might be utilized in the United States to overcome problems of valuation, capital expenditure, and relocation.

Norway enacted comprehensive new planning, building and zoning legislation in 1965, stressing strict compliance with zoning plans.[119] These plans are prepared by the municipalities, but the Ministry may require cooperation in the preparation of a zoning plan "when an area which should be considered as a unit for zoning purposes extends through several municipalities."[120] A unique feature of the Act provides that a municipal council may expropriate land for the purpose of implementing a zoning plan,[121] so long as the council "has first given the owner or lessee a reasonable period of time in which to build in accordance with the plan."[122]

This approach, permitting expropriation for any area which does not conform strictly to a zoning plan, would alleviate the necessity of demonstrating "public interest" as is required in condemnation proceedings in the U. S. Such procedures would significantly reduce the excessive time required to condemn property in this country.

Under the 1965 Act, an applicant for a building permit may be given expropriation powers when the building council stipulates that he "acquire minor parcels of unbuilt land in order to give the plot a more suitable boundary or form."[123] Within this context, "unbuilt land" may include land with buildings or structures.[124] When a municipality expropriates residential land, compensation in the form of "another residential plot in

55

the vicinity" is encouraged.[125]

Only about 10 percent of all publicly acquired land actually goes through expropriation procedures.[126] There are two reasons for this: First, the threat of expropriation tends to encourage "voluntary" sales; and second, profits from a sale of land under these circumstances are taxed at a reduced rate of about 2.5 percent. Thus, the seller may realize as much as 50 percent more "in-pocket profit" than he would in a comparable sale to a private party.[127]

National Planning

There is great concern for guiding future growth in Norway, and the country is presently operating under a "Long Term Programme 1966-69." This four-year plan resulted from the preparation of comprehensive national guidelines based on the establishment of detailed objectives and programs for each individual sector of the economy; e.g., education, fishing, electricity supply, wholesale and retail trade, housing, social policies, cultural affairs, etc. The individual programs were then translated into a coordinated economic action plan prepared with an eye to both national and international economic activities.

The Programme stresses regional planning and development, and hopes to moderate growth of the heavily populated Oslo area by following a "constructive decentralization policy." The government takes an active part in the housing problem, and expects to finance, during the four year period, approximately two-thirds of all apartments to be constructed.[128] Other basic objectives of the Programme are to provide full employment, and to achieve more even economic development throughout the different parts of the country.

Planning for Oslo

A comprehensive master plan has been prepared for Oslo and the surrounding areas. Of the total city area of 175 square miles, only about one-third is scheduled for development.[129] The remainder, which consists primarily of forests, lakes and rivers, will be retained in its natural state and utilized as recreational areas.

The plan calls for limiting population at approximately 600,000, a figure that will be reached in perhaps 15 years. At that time a choice will be made as to whether the urban density should be increased, or whether another solution is required. The plan is divided into "center," "inner," and "outer" zones. In the center zone most of the land is zoned for specific commercial uses, except for public buildings, parks, and some industrial areas. In this section some 64 percent of the land is reserved for commercial uses, and only seven percent is allocated for residential purposes. Building heights are limited to five stories, and a "floor space index" is used to establish maximum building densities.[130]

The inner zone also requires specific land uses, which are residential for the most part. The plan provides for specific types of dwellings and for maximum densities, usually on a block-by-block basis.

Plans for the outer zone were designed to preserve the character of districts where settlement already existed, but in addition provided for completely new "suburban town" residential sections for the agricultural areas south and east of Oslo. These "new towns" are based on a "modified form of the garden city idea," and are said to resemble the British new communities. They are fairly homogeneous and self-contained, complete with schools, shops, services and industry. Within each town, dwellings are arranged in small neighborhoods of perhaps 500 families. The towns are separated from one another by woods and "greenbelts," but are connected by the "Turvei" (tour way) system. A population of 15,000 − 20,000 is considered ideal for these "suburb towns."[131]

Due to topography, the traffic system is often the deciding factor in the design of a suburb town. Roadways are planned and strictly controlled according to their use. Population densities also vary in relation to the traffic system, declining progressively as one moves away from the local town center or railway station. Thus the towns have successive "rings" of apartment buildings, terrace housing and detached dwellings.

Since World War II, Oslo has played a very important role in its own development. The city has acquired a great deal of land, most of which has been leased out to private enterprise for residential and other purposes. On occasion the municipality has planned development itself, and it frequently has sought to coordinate private activities through the systematic planning of roads, railways, public utilities and services so as to provide such facilities as cheaply as possible.

One question which has not been completely resolved is the house versus apartment problem. The widespread use of apartment buildings was necessary following the war, but the feeling now is that most people would prefer to live in single-family dwellings with their own grounds and gardens. This may cause future problems due to the shortage of building land and the economies of apartment building. At present most construction is financed with loans from the State Housing Bank (and guaranteed by the Municipality) at interest rates far lower than can be found on the free market.

SWEDEN

Sweden has developed several sophisticated and uniquely effective approaches to planning in general, and expropriation in particular. Under the leasehold system, Stockholm is able to operate much like a private developer in the United States.

In the early 1900's Stockholm began a program of buying up agricultural land outside the old city, in anticipation of future expansion. Purchase money was borrowed on the open market. The land purchased was then leased out for farming until needed for development. Rents were used to pay interest on the borrowed capital. Land within the municipal boundaries was also purchased as it became available, with the result that Stockholm today owns 36 percent of the land within its municipal boundaries, and 83 percent of the property surrounding Stockholm.[132] The actual administration of the city's land program is run by STRADA, Ltd., a city-owned real estate company that operates like a private concern. The board of directors consists of five full-time commissioners, who are professional politicians.[133]

The Leasehold System

The city of Stockholm has retained nearly all land purchased over the years, preferring to lease it out under long term contracts. As a result, about 70 percent of the dwellings on the outskirts of town are built on leased land owned by the city.[134] Under new legislation passed in 1953, leasehold contracts — formerly of 60 to 100 years duration — were made valid for an "unlimited time." There are termination provisions, however, and the Act also provides for regular 10 or 20-year adjustments of ground rents.

From the municipal point of view, there are several advantages to the leasehold system. As owner of the land in fee, with a termination power over leasehold contracts, government is free to make dynamic changes in its land development patterns without resorting to expropriation procedures. In Sweden, expropriation is extremely complex and time consuming. Planning for new development has been facilitated, and made more effective on lands already owned by the city. It is doubtful whether new communities such as Vallingby and Farsta could have become a reality had the needed land been held in fragmented private ownership.

Another important advantage is that the leasehold system permits the municipality to reap inflationary profits that would otherwise accrue to private land speculators. It is felt that individual owners should not receive the benefits of "undeserved increase of land value."[135]

Zoning

Zoning controls are generally quite rigid in Sweden, as they are in many countries of Western Europe. This has led to several interesting variations from common land use practices. Under the Building Act, if a town plan includes a "special plan for the ground division" of a particular plot, and parcels of the plot are in the hands of different owners, the owner of the parcel with the "highest value" can acquire compulsorily the other parcels for development in accordance with the plan. Should this owner choose not to exercise his privilege, it then passes on to the owner of the parcel with the next highest value, and so on.[136]

The owner of a plot included in a detailed town plan is expected to comply strictly with the plan, even if this requires the demolition of existing improvements. Failure to comply within one year gives the municipality an automatic right of expropriation.[137] In practice this power is seldom utilized, however, due to budgetary limitations. Under this scheme, a Zone Expropriation clause provides for the acquisition of lands adjacent to redevelopment plots, so the municipality may realize the anticipated increase in values.

The Compensation Problem

Under the Building Act, private owners are required to sell at market value when their lands are expropriated. Because land prices tend to jump when a plan for redevelopment of an area has been adopted, Parliament was persuaded to enact an amendment which provides that the city of Stockholm may acquire the land it needs for renewal *before* it has settled on a specific plan. This amendment, passed in 1953, has proved to be of basic importance in keeping land prices within reason.[138]

Sweden provides a special judiciary body, the Court of Expropriation, which fixes the amount of compensation for both landowners and tenants. The proceedings are often quite lengthy. A dissatisfied owner has the right to lodge a protest against the compensation set, first with the Court of Appeals and thereafter with the Supreme Court. This procedure occurs regularly, since under Swedish law the local authority is liable for all the legal costs incurred by the dispossessed party in both the original and appellate courts. This provision operates whether or not the former owner's appeal is successful.[139]

The reason that expropriation procedures are so prolonged is that title to the property does not vest in the municipality until the case has proceeded to final judgement in the courts, and the compensation assessed has been deposited with the proper authorities.[140] An exception exists under a special provision of the Zone Expropriation law, however, which permits the city to take possession immediately at the onset of the proceedings. This device, called "prior admittance," requires the city to make a formal guarantee that it will pay the former owner whatever compensatory fee is established by the court, plus interest at a rate of six percent.[141] Under this procedure, the city is bound to continue its claim for the compulsory purchase. This is considered a serious disadvantage from the municipal standpoint, for under normal procedures it is possible to withdraw a compulsory purchase claim even after the case has gone to the Supreme Court.

Expropriation for Building Preservation

Under a recent amendment to the Expropriation Act, the government may expropriate noteworthy buildings or monuments in order to preserve them.[142] This law was passed to enable the city of Stockholm to preserve its historic Old Town section. Generally, however, it is applicable to "interesting building groups" in many situations. "The idea is not to preserve the buildings as museums but to repair the interior in a very careful way, thus making it possible for residents of today to live in an old milieu."[143]

A Swedish Solution to Relocation

Due to the complex interworkings of the leasehold system, owners or tenants deposed under municipal land acquisition programs are encouraged to stay on as new tenants under a lease contract. This might happen, for example, when a private owner refuses or is unable to redevelop his property in accordance with a Town or Master plan. Under threat of expropriation, the municipality may purchase and clear the land, and lease it back to the former owner. Relieved of demolition and clearing costs, the previous owner is then able to finance a new building using his compensatory fee as down payment. Both parties come out ahead. Similarly, the owners of business enterprises frequently surrender their premises when assured of a tenancy in the building to be constructed. Tenancies in new buildings are said to be in great demand.[144]

City Planning In Stockholm

Most planning decisions in the Stockholm region can be traced back to the determination, made by the City Council in 1941, that future development would be directed along the lines of a proposed underground railway system. This decision has had an important influence on the new-town planning schemes which have since been designed for municipally owned land on the city's outskirts. The theory is that the underground lines, in order to be used to their best advantage, should pass directly through the center of the built-up areas. Motor routes, on the other hand, are designed to by-pass the suburban developments by being located in the greenbelts which separate the railway lines. The total concept involves a series of alternating greenbelt corridors and built-up ribbons, all radiating out from the city center in a "finger plan."

The location of an underground line, therefore, determines the location of future development. A small local center is created around each railway station. High-rise apartment buildings are constructed within 550 yards from the station exits, while rings of terrace and detached houses are found farther out, up to a distance of 1000 yards. Generally, a suburb of this type has a population of 10-15,000 persons.

A "main center," developed around the station considered to have the most favorable situation, serves several such suburb towns. It is felt that a main center should support a population of 50,000 to 100,000 in order to function efficiently.

Since 1948, some 18 suburban units have been completed, housing a total population of more than one-quarter million. At present, three main centers are essentially completed, a fourth is well under way, and a fifth is in the advanced planning stages.[145]

Parallel with the expansion of outlying districts, a large-scale redevelopment program has also been underway in the heart of Stockholm. The first stage, a commercial center at Hötorget, is a spectacular achievement. After nearly two decades of work, it was completed in 1962. At the heart of the center five 18-story office buildings were constructed, while combined two-story structures house supporting shops, restaurants and other business facilities. A spacious central pedestrian mall, planted terraces, and a planned "open look" combine to provide unique architectural beauty. Convenient underground railway stations are found at each end of the center, and underground parking facilities are also provided.

To the south, the pedestrian mall opens out on a new two-level square, Sergels Torg. The upper level is designed for vehicular traffic, while the lower, containing shops, restaurants, and exhibition facilities, is reserved exclusively for pedestrians.[146]

Regional Planning

A regional plan for the Stockholm area was approved in 1958 by the 46 municipalities, including the city itself, in the County of Stockholm. The area covered by the plan is roughly 100 miles long by 70 miles wide. The extensive land acquisition program undertaken by the city was a major factor in creating the need for a regional plan, since portions of the land purchased overlapped into different municipalities. The need for municipal cooperation and coordination became acute as development began to take place in these outlying districts.

A high degree of autonomy is found in Swedish municipalities, and the regional plan is primarily intended to encourage planning coordination for functions that overlap political boundaries. The plan is fairly detailed for areas that are already built-up, and in addition has set out the basic features of the finger-like radial ribbons which converge on the center of the city. For the most part, however, specific implementation of the plan is left to the individual municipalities. Since the original plan was approved ten years ago, most changes in it have tended to increase the land area covered by the plan, but to decrease the physical detail provided.[147]

National Planning

There is no national planning in Sweden as such, although a new Ministry of Planning has been proposed. In reality, however, a great deal of functional planning is carried out at the State level. Planning for education, power supply, communications, the trunk road network, and many other such functions takes place on a national scale. In addition, state financial aid plays a vital part in the development of both residential and commercial facilities. About 95 percent of all dwellings in the new suburban towns have been financed with public aid. Of these, about one-third were built by city corporations, another third by co-operatives and non-profit organizations, and less than one-third by private builders.[148]

In Summary

The planning function in Sweden offers little that is new or unique. It has been said that if you ask a typical Swedish town planner what ideas have stimulated his work, he will probably name (among others): Lewis Mumford and his *Culture of Cities*, Sir Patrick Abercrombie and his *London Plan*, and Clarence S. Stein and his *Toward New Towns for America*.[149]

Why, then, has the development of the Stockholm region been such a spectacular success? Why was Stockholm awarded, in 1961, the International Union of Architects' prize, and held out as "an example to all other cities" due to its "foresight in land policy and intelligent co-ordination of the many problems confronting the modern city"?

There are, of course, a variety of reasons, but the one that sticks out above all the rest is "the municipal land policy: The city acquired large tracts of land at an early stage, and therefore it has been able to lead building development along rational lines, in accordance with its general planning policy."[150] The land banking device, new legislation enabling municipalities to extend their expropriation powers in order to implement planning schemes, and extensive use of the leasehold system have been the key factors in the successful development of the Stockholm region.

FINLAND

The Finns have a strong tradition of private land ownership. In contrast with England, Sweden, Norway, Holland and other European countries, there is at present no expropriation legislation in Finland. Thus, municipalities are forced to bargain for land in the marketplace. If necessary, it is possible to expropriate land through a special two-thirds vote of the Finnish parliament, but this obviously is an awkward and inefficient procedure.[151]

Mr. Olavi Lindblom, Director General of the State Housing Board (ARAVA), observed that "municipalities must have the right to expropriate but it must be voluntary." The Finnish constitution is a hinderance to expropriation procedures, and it is felt that the public will not accept expropriation legislation. Mr. Lindblom feels that "taxation procedures" would be more acceptable. Under the proposed procedure, taxes would be increased on profits derived from the sale of land. The tax monies would be placed in a special fund administered by local government. This fund would then be used to acquire land at fair market value. Compared to Sweden, the Netherlands, and Belgium, this is a real soft sell approach, and illustrates the wide variety of approaches to land assembly.

Land planning is beginning to gain momentum, but as yet is not widespread at any level. Regional and municipal planning, on a purely voluntary basis, is being encouraged and coordinated by the National Planning Office. All such plans must be approved by the Ministry of the Interior, but very few have been completed. In short, most planning in Finland is an *ad hoc*, voluntary function of local government.[152]

The most significant element of national intervention in planning has been in the field of low-income housing subsidies. These usually consist of long term loans with very low interest rates, which may cover as much as 60 percent of the cost of constructing rental housing.[153]

In practice, however, such loans amount to only 35-50 percent of the production costs, and have provided for only 17 percent of the total housing production.[154] This figure is actually somewhat lower than it was even a decade before, although there are plans to increase the allotment of state subsidies.

Finland is still sparsely settled, and the primary reason that planning is not widespread is that, at least until recently, there simply hasn't been a great need for it. The need is now becoming apparent as several areas have become quite highly urbanized. Housing is becoming a critical problem in some cities, and the establishment of a Central Housing Board is contemplated.

Most city land is privately owned. As the housing market expanded, the price of urban land rose some 700 percent in Helsinki from 1954 to 1960.[155] It is expected that some device will be needed to check this trend if land prices continue to rise sharply. Municipalities have tried to initiate land acquisition programs, but financial difficulties have prevented them from accomplishing much.

BELGIUM

Following the lead of several other European countries, the Belgian government began to experiment with "supramunicipal planning" soon after World War II. Studies of large urban areas such as Brussels were undertaken during the next decade. In 1958 the Ministry of Public Works Town Planning Board divided the entire country into some twenty regions for purposes of further study.[156] Twelve groups of specialists were assigned to prepare "layout plans" for each region,[157] most of which have now been completed. Since 1962 the administration has been preparing "district plans," which "are more detailed and more complete than the structure plans for the regions."[158]

In 1962 a new Expropriation Law was enacted to encourage implementation of completed plans.[159] Several features of this legislation contrast sharply with condemnation procedures in the United States. A municipality can legally take possession of condemned property within three months after initiating expropriation proceedings.[160] In practice, however, it usually takes about six months. This is still remarkable. The key to speeding up the expropriation process is that costs are negotiated *after* possession has been taken by the government.

The prepossession procedure is quite simple. The municipality prepares a plan and submits it to the County Council. The Councils are "rather close to the people," as there are some 2500 county administrative units in Belgium.[161] The County Council has 30 days in which to approve or reject the plan. Public hearings, a fixture under older expropriation procedures, are not required under the 1962 legislation. If approved, a "Royal decree" is obtained, and the owner is informed that his property has been expropriated.

The owner has recourse to the courts, where the plan, the royal decree and testimony of expert witnesses will be taken into consideration. The municipality will take possession, however, if the courts have not reached an adverse decision within 40 days. The entire procedure, except for later price negotiations, takes a maximum of six months even when judicial review is invoked.

Compensation

Belgian expropriation procedures are unique in the criteria used to determine compensation. The amount of compensation is established by a Notar, who is an expert assessor in the Ministry of Finance. A committee of civil servants appointed by the King assures honest evaluation. Fair market value is the governing principle for establishing indemnity. The criteria used to set this figure, however, are somewhat broader in scope than those utilized in the United States. After evaluating the land and buildings expropriated, the Notar will consider moving expenses and, in the case of commercial properties, good will. In addition, he may take into account such factors as interest, "disturbance" and "reinvestment" costs, so that the expenses of re-establishing a business identical to that which has been expropriated will be fully covered.

According to Mr. Wastiels, Chief Attorney for the Ministry of Public Works, the comparatively generous compensation settlements are "sophisticated in terms of people's needs, and generally work very well."[162] In fact, about the only public criticism of the expropriation process is made by the Socialist Party, which claims that property owners frequently receive *too much* compensation.

Mr. Wastiels estimated that 98 percent of all expropriation cases are not taken to court, despite the fact that the municipality must pay litigation costs for those that are. The Belgian experience demonstrates that public acquisition of private land can be both swift and socially acceptable when supported by simplified condemnation legislation and the payment of fair compensation.

Planning in Belgium

Belgium's Town and Country Planning legislation was revised extensively in 1962. Under the new amendments, every municipality (except those with less than 1,000 population) is required to prepare a detailed "layout plan."[163] The municipalities also draw up their own building regulations, although this function is subject to state direction and unification for "large urban areas." Completed layout plans are submitted to the Town Planning Board for approval. Municipal plans are prepared, not only according to economic and social criteria, but also from an "esthetic point of view, in order to preserve the country's beautiful scenery."[164]

Municipal boards issue building and "parcelling" permits for development in accordance with their layout plans. A board can issue a permit even if no plan has been approved, but in this situation the Town Planning Board can overrule the decision using its "advisory right of interference." The Town Board also has power to suspend any permit improperly granted, regardless of whether or not a layout plan has been approved.

Once a layout plan has been approved, the power to expropriate becomes general, to the effect that any "destination" given a property by the plan may be enforced by law. Within a territory included in a general layout plan, more detailed special plans are often drawn up. One type that is used rather widely is the "restricted special plan," which usually is used to "reparcel" properties among the existing owners. These "alignment plans," as they are also called, are designed to redistribute land in a manner designed to facilitate conformance with the general layout plan.

Regional and district plans are prepared by the State. There is a distinct effort made to impart the highest possible degree of flexibility to the plans prepared at each level. A municipal plan, under certain circumstances, may modify some provisions of a district plan. Certain deviations from the requirements of a special layout plan are also possible.

The last of the twenty regional plans, which tend to be economically oriented, was completed in 1967. Planners are now at work on about three dozen district plans which cover major subdivisions within the regions. The district plans will be more detailed than the regional plans.

THE NETHERLANDS

Land use control legislation in the Netherlands dates back to the Housing Act of 1901.[165] The Act required municipalities to establish local building regulations, and to prepare "extension plans" for future growth areas. This legislation has provided the basis for the development of tight governmental control over all land use. It has resulted in detailed development plans for most municipalities, and has been extended to cover the regional planning program.[166]

In the Netherlands, no new construction or structural improvements can be undertaken without a permit. Permits will be issued only if the request conforms to both the town plan and the "minutely detailed" municipal building codes.[167] In addition, owners of existing structures may be required to execute improvements designated by the municipality. If they fail to do so, the improvements may be made and charged to the owner, or the building may be condemned.[168]

The Netherlands also has a large-scale and flexible system for financing and subsidizing housing construction. The system operates almost exclusively at the national level, and is available to both public and private builders. Aid may take the forms of loans, annual subsidies or lump-sum contributions.[169]

Comprehensive planning in the Netherlands achieves the opposite effect of zoning in the United States. In the U.S. a landowner is free to develop his own property as he wishes, subject only to specific governmental restrictions. The Dutch, however, *prohibit* any building on land which has not been specifically designated for building purposes.[170] The Dutch land use control measures eliminate the need for "zoning."

Expropriation Procedures

Regarding land assembly specifically, the Dutch expropriation procedures are similar in many ways to those found in Belgium. The key to the determination of fair compensation is that "personal financial status should not be altered."[171] Compensation is based on current market value of the property taken, including any "anticipatory value" due to advantageous physical location with respect to existing development plans. In the case of industrial or commercial displacement, the award includes moving expenses, loss of income, and the cost of higher operating expenses at the replacement site.

One other factor, called "tax damage," illustrates how comprehensive the compensation determination is. Property taxes are established for entire areas, based on similarity of uses rather than on assessment of individual sites. An owner reaps a windfall if he can derive an income from his property higher than the "normal" established for his tax area. Under the Dutch expropriation procedure the owner would be compensated even for the "tax damage" suffered in the loss of his purely fortuitous windfall.[172] The fairness of the compensation paid under the Dutch expropriation process has resulted in far less controversy and public resistance than we are accustomed to in the United States.

1962 Planning Legislation

After operating under the 1901 planning laws for more than 60 years, the Dutch enacted comprehensive new planning and housing legislation in 1962. Many Dutch planners felt their country was ready for a detailed national plan, which would incorporate regional and local plans into a broad framework defining the physical development and planning objectives of the nation as a whole. An elaborate draft bill for such legislation was prepared.[173]

The bill, however, was not successful. After "ample reflection," it was decided that the rigidity of such a scheme would provide too little elasticity. Therefore new legislation was designed, containing "a degree of flexibility" in order that development regulations might be adjusted to "often rapidly changing circumstances."[174]

Under the new scheme, the main emphasis is placed — as it always was — on municipal development plans. A municipality can set up three types of plans: a master plan for its entire area, a development plan for the territory outside its built-up area, and another development plan for its built-up area. The master plan is actually a broad program to guide future development. It is not detailed, in a physical sense, and does not contain binding regulations. Several municipalities may set up a master plan "in concert."

The development plans, on the other hand, are quite detailed. A plan for territory outside the built-up area establishes specific uses for all land and buildings within its range. Such a plan, which is merely a continuation of the "extension plan" concept found in the 1901 legislation, is required of every municipality. These plans have the force of law, and all future development must conform to the detailed requirements of the plans. Since the plans have such binding force, public hearings are required before a plan is "made definite" by the municipal council. An aggrieved party may appeal to the provincial government, and ultimately to the "Crown," if he feels his objections to the plan have not been given proper consideration. Once approved, however, the plan is practically inviolable.

The concept of a development plan encompassing the built-up area, however, is new. Such plans were not provided for under the older legislation. It was felt that redevelopment plans are needed to check haphazard clearing and reconstruction in existing parts of towns, and to "tie in" such projects with a program involving the entire municipal area. The preparation of such plans poses special problems because, even though they must be extremely detailed, a degree of flexibility must also be retained. The solution now being explored is to prepare a plan which is essentially a cross between a "master" plan and a "development" plan. The objective is to provide defined goals and objectives for a large area, to be filled in with detailed plans for smaller areas as the need for reconstruction arises. Building permits are "frozen" while a detailed area plan is being prepared, which may take as long as three years.

1962 Housing Act

The new Housing Act differs from the 1901 legislation mainly in the emphasis which has now been placed on the responsibility of the national government in housing matters.[175] The Act consists basically of three separate sections. The first establishes a number of criteria to be satisfied by the individual municipal building codes. Previously, each municipality had developed its own set of detailed building regulations independently. Discrepancies from one code to another were wide and varied. The new Housing Act attempts to promote uniformity, in order to facilitate the development of new technologies, and also to satisfy the craftsmen who were forced to work with an existing potpourri of confusing and sometimes conflicting rules and regulations.

The second part of tne new Act is concerned with the elimination of unfit housing conditions. Under this section, municipal officials can order a property owner to carry out designated improvements. The owner is obligated either to make the improvements or vacate the building. If he fails to comply, the municipality may have the improvements made, charging the cost to the owner, or else the dwelling may be condemned.

The third section of the Act provides "an extensive complex of legal provisions and rules"[176] dealing with governmental financing and subsidies for home construction. Under these provisions, financial aid is available to housing associations, municipalities private builders and individuals; aid may be in the form of loans, annual or lump-sum contributions. Loans may be acquired to cover as much as the complete building cost of a dwelling, while contributory aid is used to make up deficits in operating revenues and expenses. The effect of the national housing program is substantial. In 1966, the government financed the construction of some 125,000 dwelling units, of which nearly half were built by housing associations and municipalities.[177]

PUERTO RICO

A statewide Land Authority has assembled and controlled land in Puerto Rico for many years.[178] Most of the prime agricultural lands are owned by American sugar interests. The Land Authority was created to prevent the further formation of huge plantations, and to protect local agricultural interests from the giant American corporations.

The Authority has very broad powers.[179] It is authorized to acquire and manage lands, commercial interests, factories and other related facilities. It may loan money for private development. The Authority can dispose of, or lease out, any properties which it does not wish to operate itself. In addition, it is authorized to hold stock in private corporations, and on occasion operates farms or commercial facilities on a "partnership" basis with private interests. In general, the Land Authority has been given the freedom and flexibility to function in whatever manner will best serve the interests of the Puerto Rican agricultural economy.

The eminent domain procedure available to the Land Authority is particularly interesting, since it functions within an essentially "Americanized" legal system. Under this process, the Authority determines what it considers to be fair value for the property to be taken. Notice is filed, and the suggested compensation is paid into the court.[180] Title vests in the Land Authority at that time, although the compensation offered is subject to re-evaluation and a final determination at a later date.[181] The court, after examining the individual interests involved, establishes a date for actual change of possession.[182] After the date set, the Authority is free to improve or demolish existing structures even though a final judgment regarding compensation has not yet been reached.[183]

---

[97] "Betterment" consists of an increase in land value due to a change in use. If, for example, a developer purchased a run-down residential property in order to construct a high-rise apartment building, the difference in the value of the land for the proposed commercial use versus the existing residential use is "betterment." Under the 1947 Act, the tax was 100% of such difference in value.

[98] See Heap, *Introducing the Land Commission Act* (London, 1967). The author, Desmond Heap, Comptroller and City Solicitor of London, is recognized as a leading authority on land use planning. This book presents an excellent balance between commentary and the enabling legislation itself.

[99] See Note 97 for an illustration of "betterment." The levy is to be 40% of the development value of the land but the Government intends that this figure shall be increased progressively (and at reasonably short intervals) to 45% and then to 50% with a reserve power being vested in the Land Commission to increase the rate still further if it so desires (White Paper, para. 30).

[100] The Land Commission Bill § 7-A, (Her Majesty's Stationery Office, London, 1965) [hereinafter cited Land Commission Bill].

[101] Land Commision Bill, § 11.

[102] Interview with G. Chipperfield, Ministry of Housing and Local Government, London, England, October 13, 1967.

[103] Interview with Wyndham Thomas and Sir Henry Wells, London, England, Oct. 13, 1967.

references/footnotes

[104] Address by Sir Henry Wells, before the Rating and Valuation Association, Oct. 16, 1967.

[105] Address by Sir Henry Wells, before the Association of Land and Property Owners, May 8, 1967.

[106] Address by Sir Henry Wells, before the Metropolitan Association of Building Societies, Oct. 17, 1967.

[107] Land Commission Bill, § 15.

[108] Land Commission Bill, § 14.

[109] Land Commission Bill, § 18.

[110] Land Commission Bill, § 19.

[111] *Ibid.*

[112] Land Commission Bill, § 21.

[113] Land Commission Bill, § 22.

[114] Address by Sir Henry Wells, before the Metropolitan Association of Building Societies, Oct. 17, 1967.

[115] Address by Sir Henry Wells, before the Association of Municipal Corporations Conference, September 20, 1967.

[116] Prof. Lichfield very kindly consented to review the first draft of all the English materials, and his corrections, criticisms and additions have proved invaluable.

[117] Interview with Prof. Nathaniel Lichfield, London, England, Oct. 12, 1967.

[118] Interview with Wyndham Thomas and Sir Henry Wells, London, England, Oct. 13, 1967.

[119] The Building Act of 18th of June, 1965.

[120] The Building Act, § 30.

[121] The Building Act, § 35 (1).

[122] The Building Act, § 35 (3).

[123] The Building Act, § 39 (2).

[124] The Building Act, § 39 (3).

[125] The Building Act, § 44.

[126] Interview with Jens Seip, Deputy Director, State Housing Bank, and Ingvar Tofte, Ministry of Municipal Affairs and Labor, Oslo, Norway, Oct. 15, 1967.

[127] *Ibid.*

[128] Norwegian Long Term Programme 1966-1969, p. 14.

[129] Town Planning Dept., Oslo Planning and Development (1967), p. 4.

[130] *Ibid.* p. 5.

[131] *Ibid.* p. 8.

[132] Interview with Lars Wunge, Real Estate Department, Stockholm, Sweden, Oct. 17, 1967.

[133] *Ibid.*

[134] Folke Lundin, *The Application of the Leasehold System in Stockholm, Sweden*, p. 4.

[135] Westman, *Memorandum Relating to Zone Expropriation on Lower Norrmalm in Stockholm* (1967), p. 3.

[136] Building Act of June 30, 1947, § 46.

[137] Building Act of June 30, 1947, § 44.

[138] Holmgren, *About Town Planning In Sweden* (1967), p. 5.

[139] Westman, *Memorandum Relating to Zone Expropriation on Lower Norrmalm in Stockholm* (1967), p. 3.

[140] *Ibid.* at 4.

[141] *Ibid.*

[142] Expropriation Act of May 12, 1917, § 1 (12).

[143] Commentary on the Expropriation Act, p. 6.

[144] Westman, *Memorandum Relating to Zone Expropriation on Lower Norrmalm in Stockholm*, p. 6.

[145] Much of the information found above was taken from Holmgren, *About Town Planning In Sweden* (1967), pp. 8-10.

[146] *Ibid.* pp. 10-11.

[147] *Ibid.* p. 13.

[148] Sidenbladh, "Planning Problems in Stockholm," in *City Planning Commission, Stockholm: Regional and City Planning* (1964), pp. 58-59.

[149] Larsson, "Building a City and a Metropolis," in *City Planning Commission, Stockholm: Regional and City Planning* (1964), p. 8.

[150] *Ibid.* p. 9.

[151] Interview with Olavi Lindblom, Director General of State Planning Board, Helsinki, Finland, Oct. 21, 1967.

[152] Hannus, *National Monograph: Finland* (1965), p: 4.

[153] *Ibid.* p. 3.

[154] *Ibid.* p. 2.

[155] *Ibid.* p. 8.

[156] *Town and Country Planning in Belgium* (1966), p. 8.

[157] *Ibid.* p. 9.

[158] *Ibid.* p. 14.

[159] Expropriation Laws of 26 July, 1962. Unfortunately, these have been printed only in French and Dutch.

[160] Interview with Ing. Wm. Platteau, Service Urbanisme, Brussels, Belgium, Oct. 25, 1967.

[161] This description of expropriation procedures is based on an interview with F. Wastiels, chief attorney, Ministry of Public Works, Brussels, Belgium, Oct. 25, 1967.

[162] Interview with F. Wastiels, chief attorney, Ministry of Public Works, Brussels, Belgium, Oct. 25, 1967.

[163] As of 1965, there were 2,588 municipalities in Belgium, of which some 1,100 had less than 1,000 residents. *Town and Country Planning in Belgium* (1966), p. 2.

[164] *Town and Country Planning in Belgium* (1966), p. 5.

[165] Bommer, *Housing and Planning Legislation in the Netherlands* (1967), p. 11.

[166] Parenthetically, it should be added that excessive application of land use controls has resulted in some dull, monotonous and over-planned examples of urban development. But this may also be a result of the Dutch character and attitudes toward land conservation and utilization.

[167] Interview with Cornelius de Cler, Chief, Town Planning Department, Ministry of Housing and Physical Planning, The Hague, Oct. 23, 1967.

[168] Bommer, *Housing and Planning Legislation in the Netherlands* (1967), pp. 22-23.

[169] *Ibid.* p. 25.

[170] Interview with Cornelius de Cler, Chief, Town Planning Department, Ministry of Housing and Physical Planning, The Hague, Oct. 23, 1967.

[171] *Ibid.*

[172] *Ibid.*

[173] Bommer, *Housing and Planning Legislation in the Netherlands* (1967), p. 14.

[174] *Ibid.*

[175] *Ibid.*, p. 21.

[176] *Ibid.*, p. 24.

[177] *Ibid.*, pp. 25-26.

[178] Laws Puerto Rico Ann. Tit. 28, § 242.

[179] The powers mentioned in this paragraph are all found in Laws Puerto Rico Ann. Tit. 28, § 261.

[180] Laws Puerto Rico Tit. 28, § 270.

[181] Laws Puerto Rico Tit. 28, § 271.

[182] Laws Puerto Rico Tit. 28, § 273.

[183] Laws Puerto Rico Tit. 28, § 275.

Chapter 5

THE EFFECT OF TECHNOLOGY
AND DESIGN ON LAND
COSTS, UTILIZATION AND ASSEMBLY

Architects, planners and housing economists frequently advocate new technology, cluster housing and mass production as methods of driving down the high cost of housing. While there is a great potential for dollar savings in new technology, there is little evidence that such savings are possible given the present state of technological development. We should not pass judgment on the ability of the American homebuilding industry to make great strides in the economic use of land and cost savings through new advances in technology and design. We need far more experience on which to base such a case.

One of the factors limiting the merchandising of new residential designs and new communities is the market. The market has not been educated or trained to appreciate, recognize and demand good community and residential design. In other industries this form of education, or persuasion, is called "demand management." The housing industry must move into the Twentieth Century. It must initiate demand management programs.

Economies of Scale

There are two key factors related to "economies of scale" in the homebuilding industry: (1) the size of the homebuilders' project, and (2) the size of the homebuilders' operation. The size of the project affects production and marketing costs. In the early 1950's the mass production techniques of the Levittowns were thought to represent a major "breakthrough." The cost savings involved in larger sites were highly exaggerated. Builders today know that these economies of scale are subject to certain definite limitations. As Ned Eichler puts it, "Although a 500 or 1,000-acre tract may offer economies of scale in site work over one of 50 or 100 acres, it is very doubtful that any economies are to be accrued from land over 1,000 acres."[184] Actually, the big merchant builder is more sensitive to the market, the cost of financing and the "lead time" on a project, than he is to economies of scale.

More important than theories is the way the merchant builders are acting. What are the present building levels of the larger developers? A few builders are still starting 2,000 or more dwelling units in a year. But they aren't all in one area as was often the case in the mid-fifties for such builders as Levitt, Aldon, Diller-Kallsman, Aetna and Grandview.[185] These builders have "psyched the market" — they reduce the margin of risk by starting projects in a number of states or areas rather than concentrating on one site or project.

Economies of scale are more significant when the size of the development company itself is considered. But this, too, is subject to certain limitations. Benefits resulting from high quality production and design may increase sales, but are not necessarily reflected in a lower per-unit cost. Further, savings that are the result of bulk purchasing, greater use of mechanical equipment, and company sales and marketing staffs, are offset by certain economies which accrue to small-scale developers. For instance, small builders' costs are substantially reduced by the use of non-union labor in certain areas, and by more efficient supervision, particularly when the builder himself is "on the job."[186]

The success story of the large-scale developer began with the housing shortage that occurred after World War II. Large builders advanced in four significant areas. They were able to (1) find land and finance its purchase at a cost savings, (2) establish smooth working arrangements with FHA and VA, (3) negotiate more forcefully with local authorities concerning zoning and utilities, and (4) create an assembly line production system. In the fourth area, mass production meant standardization and specialization of labor, increased use of power tools and equipment, and direct dealings with manufacturers of needed materials. Later advances were also made in management, accounting and marketing procedures.[187]

The lack of economies of scale beyond the 500 to 800-house range has retarded the growth of established volume builders.[188] Today the trend seems to be toward the expansion of smaller firms, rather than the increased expansion of established volume builders. "We'll be seeing and selling to more regional and national builders in the 1970's" says Richard A. Drickey, Marketing Research Manager for Whirlpool Corporation. "Efficiency can only take place if you have large builders who fan out over a region."[189]

Major corporate giants are moving into the homebuilding industry. Perhaps they will achieve greater economies of scale. Sunset International Petroleum, Humble and Christiana Oil Corporation are among the big corporations becoming involved in construction.[190] U.S. Plywood joined Jim Walter Corp. in developing a leisure home community in Texas. Penn Central railroad combined with Kaiser to develop the 87,500-acre Rancho California. Westinghouse and General Electric have launched pilot projects.[191]

Clear Lake City, planned for 180,000 people, is another illustration of this activity. Humble Oil and Refining Company had originally purchased 15,000 acres of land in 1940, 25 miles from Houston, for industrial development. When its original plans had to be scrapped in 1962, it decided to construct a "new town" because of the low land cost of $300 an acre. However, the distance factor nearly crippled the scheme. A huge advertising campaign highlighted the $1,000,000 recreation center; but only 36 people bought homes the first month. By June of 1966 a mere 625 homes had been sold.[192]

Alcoa is also involved in new large-scale development. In 1961 Alcoa purchased 260 acres of land in West Los Angeles from Twentieth Century Fox, at a cost of $43 million. This land had previously been used as a back lot location for motion picture production. Alcoa began the construction of a new in-city development called Century City on 180 acres of this site. With a multi-million dollar investment, the company is constructing homes and offices designed to accommodate a population of some 12,000 and provide working facilities for 20,000 or more people. The street pattern involves 35 acres of land in 5 miles of roadways. To provide parking space, plans call for underground parking facilities to be built for 30,000 cars. [193]

What the invasion of corporate empires means to the future of the homebuilding industry is anybody's guess. Lawrence J. Weinberg, President of Larwin Company, believes that a builder cannot do the necessary research and development work until he is building ten to fifteen thousand units a year. He also claims that major technological advances will only be possible with a production of 25,000 units a year. [194]

Technology

"It is a breathtaking site, a 100,000-acre set for a Fellini movie." The commentator was speaking of Cape Kennedy. He was viewing structures the size of 30-story office buildings, moving serenely across the landscape on wheels. He was awed by the technology at NASA missile sites which allowed prefabricated workshops and labs to be hoisted into position, plugged into prepared services and removed when no longer needed. But even more, he was excited by the possibility that this technology might be applied to urban development [195]

The widely discussed marriage of technology and urban development has yet to be consummated. The courtship began in the post-war years with the magic of prefabrication and Buckminster Fuller's dymaxion house. However, during the 1950's there were few technological innovations of significant benefit to the building trades. Improvements in production and efficiency during that time were achieved in the absence of technological advances. [196] The practical builders found the benefits of prefabrication more myth than reality. Today, builders such as Levitt say they are through with the "prefabrication mess." They still assemble some items at the plant, but the totally prefabricated house is a thing of the past. [197]

In the late 1950's the National Association of Home Builders (NAHB) predicted a trend toward improved materials and techniques. However, the NAHB said significant advances would have to wait until the big corporations get into the homebuilding field.[198] In the early 1960's many technological innovations helped the merchant builder. Earth-moving equipment was specially designed for each job, and grading became a science of its own (and a threat to the landscape, according to many architects, planners and conservationists). In addition, expandable sewage plants were developed which enabled builders to avoid large initial investments in these facilities. Builder-operated nurseries allowed expensive shade trees to be grown on idle subdivision land. Low cost street lighting and soil cement paving were also initiated.[199]

The federal government has expressed interest in applying technology to urban problems. In June of 1966, the well-publicized "Woods Hole Meeting" was held. It was sponsored by HUD, and was attended by representatives of science, industry and government. A call was made for a "giant-sized" national building research effort.[200]

The states also share in this search for large-scale economies in construction and technological breakthroughs. New Jersey is making an effort in this direction. Under the New Jersey Demonstration Grant Act, passed in 1967, the Commissioner of the Department of Community Affairs is authorized to create a revolving fund which will use financial grants to encourage innovations in new techniques and materials for housing construction and rehabilitation.[201]

In New York City, developer Warren Chalks is constructing his "Capsule Unit Tower." It is a centrally-supported structure with prefabricated "apartment capsules" of varying size, hoisted into place on the tower.[202] In Pittsburgh, the proposed Allegheny Center, a 79-acre project with 1,300 apartments and 220 town houses, will have a centrally located heating and cooling system which will save space and the cost of heavy equipment duplication.[203]

In Canada, sectional houses built by Alcoa's Design Homes, Ltd. are another striking innovation. J.C. Neely, president of the company, claims that complete homes will be built at the factory in two main sections and trucked to the development site. These homes, costing an estimated $10,000, are designed to tap the low income market of persons making $5,000 or less.[204] Technology still has a long way to go to bring the home building industry into the space age. A continuing program of research and development in building technology is sorely needed. Most R & D programs to date have been one-shot, single technique projects. The president of the new State University of New York at Buffalo, Martin Meyerson, has proposed a building technology education and research program designed to bridge the technology gap. This program may have an impact on the industry, but it is still too soon to gauge that impact.

Site Planning and Open Space

Site planning can reduce the developer's land needs and costs by making more efficient use of the land, but good site planning is the exception rather than the rule. According to a recent study prepared for HUD by the Building Research Council of Illinois:

> The bulk of current site planning in the United States is of mediocre quality. Exceptions are random since they do not seem to fall into any discernable geographic pattern or relate to any particular housing program. Good practice is attributable to a combination of skillful designers and motivated developers.[205]

All too often, open space in residential projects is planned merely for its aesthetic benefits without any thought to its utilitarian aspect. For example, the Riis Houses built on New York's lower east side during the late 1940's were the pride of the New York Housing Authority. Fourteen-story apartment buildings covered only twenty percent of the land, and a beautiful view of the East River was preserved. "The rest was what the poor had always desired — open space, filled with what the planners thought they wanted, greenery." However, the fenced-in parks with keep-off-the-grass signs weren't really needed. Recently the situation was corrected. A usable park with playgrounds *and* greenery was built.[206]

Planned Unit Development

Our subdivisions of today provide little open space beyond the backyard.[207] Architects and planners often suggest planned unit development and clustering as an alternative to the dull monotony of the typical suburban subdivision.[208] PUD's, which are planned as total development units, allow for the use of flexible zoning provisions creating a variety of land use patterns. However, the lack of state legislation in the field has retarded the use of PUD. But in May of 1967, a first step was taken. New Jersey passed the nation's first Planned Unit Development law, thus forging the way into this new method of community design.[209]

The advantages of clustering are better siting, shorter streets and utility lines, less through traffic and more open space. In comparing cluster development with conventional development, the Urban Land Institute found the former required approximately twenty percent less road and utility footage and provided fifteen times as much open land. A town-house plan provides greater density while road footage is reduced by one-half and open areas are significantly increased.[210] The use of a town-house plan, as is found in the Eichler homes in Santa Clara, California, provides additional benefits. Visual spaciousness is added while the row house look is broken up. Pedestrian traffic is substantially separated from vehicular traffic.[211]

Even more dramatic is the design of Habitat for Expo '67 in Montreal. Prefabricated apartments were hoisted into position and arranged in an unusual design matrix. While the Moshe Safdie design was not a new concept, it was the first time it got off the architect's drawing board. It achieved high density housing on limited land, while maximizing individual privacy and open space in the form of large terraces. The architect's objective was to provide a sense of community while maintaining something of the space and privacy enjoyed in the suburbs.[212]

This idea of "building with boxes" has received an enthusiastic acceptance by American architects and builders in the last year. However, the concept is not without its drawbacks. "Habitat '67, which touched off the boom in box schemes, can now be seen in sharper perspective as an architecturally brilliant but technically cumbersome version of a long-established concept."[213]

Design, People and Cars

The site designer's biggest problem is providing automobile circulation and storage that does not interfere with people. A poorly planned transportation network wastes land and increases costs. There are, however, no simple solutions to the conflict between people and cars. In point of fact, the auto is a very inefficient mode of mass transportation, yet the love affair between urban man and his auto flourishes, however disfunctional it may be. This dilemma is not restricted to housing developments. The conflict also occurs in the downtown commercial areas of every major American city. Philadelphia, for instance, has been struggling with urban mass transportation since the inception of Penn Center by the Penn Central railroad.[214]

The proposed Market Street East project, covering 113 acres in the center of the city, attempts to bring the suburbs downtown and tie together Philadelphia's transportation system. Different levels of bus, subway, automobile and pedestrian traffic, with multilevel parking, integrate the transportation network with the commercial core area.

Highway and transportation policies have had a tremendous influence on how land is used. They have helped make suburban growth possible by cutting down commuting time. Highways bring more land within the reach of the developer. They also cause its misuse by encouraging premature subdivision. Obviously, what we need is a transportation system which meets the needs of the people and at the same time promotes the efficient use of the land. Of course, this is easier said than done. Balanced transportation systems have been built in the Scandinavian countries. Rapid transit and highway systems give the consumer a choice. Competition could result in mass transportation once again becoming a major factor in the urban pattern — less to reduce the use of the automobile and more to provide alternative means of movement and accessibility for the young, the old, the ill, and those who may prefer to use their automobiles to go out into the countryside rather than for daily trips to work or schools or shops.

84

Demand Management

In talking to builders and developers of new communities, it was very evident that the middle-class life style as reflected in residential consumer choice was the most critical factor in determining the type, character and layout of new suburban developments. In building trade parlance this is called, simply, "the market." Today the market has a far greater impact on the shape and content of urbanization than all our planning and zoning efforts.

New communities, town houses, cluster plans and other innovations represent a very small part of new suburban construction. It's not just that good design costs more. The consumer has not been adequately "informed," "educated," or "trained" to appreciate and buy good community design.

Architectural critic Wolf Von Eckardt observed in "The Reston Experience" that:

> The houses didn't sell as fast as they should have — the construction program lagged. In part this was due to the newness of the place. Who wants to be a pioneer? In part it was due to the tight money market. In part it was due to the expense. Reston's outstanding design and special amenities added as much as $3,000 to each house. "People," an expert told me, "would spend perhaps $1,000 more for these extras, but not $3,000."[215]

All too often the imaginative community builder is too far ahead of his market. The experienced builder knows he must build houses and communities that can be sold at a reasonable profit. There is a natural law in home merchandising that limits how far ahead of his market the builder can get. The vast majority of new subdivisions and home construction, including the so-called "pacesetters," continue to be dull, montonous and commonplace in the opinion of many planners and architects.

In testifying before the Housing Subcommittee of the House Banking and Currency Committee, Developer James W. Rouse said:

> Nor have we developed the capacity in the homebuilding industry for producing well-planned large-scale urban development. *Although the business of city building is the largest single industry in America, there is no large corporation engaged in it.* City building has no General Motors or General Electric —

no IBM, no Xerox; no big capital resources to invest in the purchase of large land areas; no big research and development program unfolding new techniques to produce a better environment."[216]

In other industries, the management of demand is an essential part of the total production process. The key is effective control of purchases by final consumers. If they are under effective control, there will be a relatively reliable demand for the raw materials going into the ultimate product. If General Motors can develop a reliable demand for automobiles, it can give its suppliers long term contracts. It can assure them there will be a continuing need for their raw materials. By stabilizing demand it can get lower prices on raw materials. If we had a few General Motors in the housing industry, they could insure that consumers spend a predictable share of their income on "GM" homes.

The control or management of demand is a new industry employing a vast network of communications, merchandising and selling organizations. It includes advertising and research training activities designed to influence consumer choice. Except for limited newspaper and radio advertising, the management of consumer demand in the homebuilding industry is still very primitive.

The homebuilding industry is composed of many small local builders, and a few big national builders, competing for a limited part of local markets. Tight competition and close margins limit the amount of "demand management" the individual builder can engage in. This raises the question of whether the industry itself might, through its various organizations such as NAHB, explore the advantages of demand management for the industry as a whole.

In Fremont, California, planning director Roy W. Potter claimed that cluster housing and green space for parks became popular.

> Once one developer had provided a common green, the competition began falling into line. People looking at houses would say, "Where's your park"? It started as a sales gimmick. But we were able to show the developer that he didn't lose any units and at the same time saved money on utilities and street

costs. Since then over 15 planned unit developments have been built in Fremont, and the population tripled from 21,00 to 63,000 [217]

Exploration into demand management in the homebuilding industry also provides a fertile field for the intellectual community which has probed and analyzed negative land use controls in great detail. Indeed, the trend among planning and zoning experts today is to advocate compensation to land owners for losses due to zoning changes. Zoning is negative, and can be socially regressive. We have not been able to develop any other device to keep the "pig out of the parlor" — to keep the tannery out of the R-1 residential neighborhood.

Demand management, on the other hand, might provide a creative outlet for promoting new community design concepts on a nationwide basis. On this scale, persuasion would require wide-ranging and compelling communication between the managers and the managed. Such communication and persuasion must hold the attention of the consumer for considerable periods of time, in a subtle and relaxed manner. It must reach all levels of the market. With more and more families making more and more money, and the prospect of a continuing rise in the Gross National Product, an increasingly large part of the population could be persuaded to buy better community design.

Up to now the advertising media has concentrated on smaller, disposable goods from toothpaste to automobiles. Housing needs and community design desires have been totally unmanaged. Today television has become one of the prime instruments for consumer demand. As John Kenneth Galbraith points out:

> The industrial system is profoundly dependent on commercial television and could not exist in its present form without it. Economists who eschew discussion of its economic significance, or dismiss it as a wicked waste, are protecting their reputation and that of their subject for Calvinistic austerity. But they are not adding to their reputation for relevance. [218]

It seems clear that we now live in a national economy. Motivation studies indicate housing preferences are subject to regional tastes and influences. Deep research into the

87

motivations of home buyers is not needed. The merchant builder has been doing this for years. What is needed is a strategy of demand management. We have developed an enormous industry for advertising — newspapers, magazines, radio and, most important, television. This new industry is constantly looking for new clients. It seems evident that a national approach to well-designed new communities might provide a fertile field for the advertising industry. It is important to remember, however, that people probably need to believe that they are unmanaged if they are to be managed effectively. We like to think that we have maximum freedom of choice. If the American consumer were to recognize the degree to which he is subjected to demand management, it might result in a consumer revolution.

However, since there are no clear-cut limits in the amount of demand management to which the public will respond, the homebuilding industry today has tremendous latitude. Well-designed communities are a new product which will require new merchandising techniques.

If modern industrial techniques are going to be applied to housing and urbanization, then demand management should be included. The objectives should be improving consumer knowledge regarding alternative patterns of urban life, the advantages of new communities, and how the consumer can get better housing and neighborhood values for his dollar.

Rising Expectations

We have discussed the sound and the fury regarding the unrest, discontent and rising expectations of the poor, but rising middle-class expectations may have as profound an impact on the quality as well as the quantity of our new urban environment, if not a greater one.

The manipulation of demand management is also extending into urban politics. As Columbia political scientist Zbigniew Brzezinski has observed:

> Traditional urban political elites are increasingly replaced by professional political leadership possessing special technical skills, relying on intellectual talents and exploiting mass media

to mobilize individual support directly, no longer by the intermediary of organized parties.[219]

The expanded application of demand management by industry and increased exploitation of mass media by urban politicians does not imply a grim and meaningless utopia, populated by pre-programmed masses. Rather, it means greater opportunity for direct market feed-back to industry and policy makers — the builders and the politicians.

In the industrial age, human experience was largely characterized by scarcity for the middle class and deprivation for the poor. According to many social philosophers, we have now emerged into the post-industrial age. In the post-industrial age the struggle to make a living will be replaced by affluent societies, with many new choices of life-style available. This transition has intriging implications for reforming the urban environment and upgrading the quality of urban life. As long as the quest for individual material progress dominated society, the concept of community and the public interest suffered. The arguments for conservation and an attractive, healthy environment were written by intellectuals or well-to-do dilettantes — but substantive achievements were few. It could be said that, according to the middle class, the most beautiful thing in the world was a buck, not a tree. As one conservationist summed it up, "If you scratch the heart of almost any American, you will find a trace of the land speculator."

As long as scarcity, deprivation and the economic hustle were prime movers, the quality of environment received scant attention at the national level. (President Johnson's wife was given the responsibility for "urban beautification.") But now the victory of science and technology heralds the coming of the "technotronic society." Material abundance assures the security of urban man and makes Marx's "economic man" irrelevant and obsolete. It does not matter who owns the engines of production — Socialist managers or Capitalist managers — they are equally suspect. The executive vice-president of the nation's biggest bank and the president of a large university have both been impressed by the realization that:

89

... the major issues facing the country were not so much quantitative as qualitative. Young people literally rebelled against the success of our economy. It is not surprising that they are now looking at the ideals, at the qualitative aspects of life — the peace, tranquility, cultural relations, the effort to clean up polluted air, water, congestion, noise, and all of this. At a time when all the resources are pretty much committed, we are faced with people asking for more.[220]

Martin Meyerson, President of the State University of New York at Buffalo, observed that:

Much of what disturbs intellectuals, protesting students, and spokesmen for the black and the poor also disturbs a large bloc of American conservatives. They all are suspicious about the corruption and bureaucracy of big government, big unions, and big corporations. They all see moral deficit and hypocrisy in the regulations, red tape, ineptitude, and lack of responsibility which they believe accompany large-scale bureaucracies of any kind.[221]

With the rising expectations of the post-industrial epoch, the agenda of human concern may rapidly shift from the pursuit of money to the quality of urban life. In fact, the intellectuals, artists, protesting college students and to some extent, militant blacks, have already made the transition. They are now far more concerned with "giving life meaningful content," with art, music, movies and other creative and sensual uses of leisure. They reject the economic treadmill. They are "turned on" by contemplative and hedonistic delights, much of it fashionable and trivial but a social indicator or bellwether of future trends nevertheless. This concern — the creative use of leisure and increasing affluence — with arts and crafts, painting and sculpture can, and will, lead to larger environmental concerns such as architecture, community design and conservation. These were not the driving, motivating forces of a commercialized-industrialized society, but if the great middle class (Nixon's "forgotten man") follows the lead of the artist-intellectual, the public concept of community will inevitably change. The joys of clean air, water and landscape will find an increased consituency if middle-class man begins to seek the kind of society and environment that heretofore only utopians could envision.

In Summary

A large-scale developer tends to utilize better site design and provide more open space. Beyond certain limits, however, there are no cost savings. The big builders may have reached the optimum size in terms of economies of scale. Technological advances may reduce development costs and allow a developer to make more efficient use of land in the future. However, we have yet to see any major technological breakthroughs in the housing industry. Good site design can conserve land, but land conservation and site design are generally dictated by what sells.

Technology, design and economies of scale could substantially affect the efficiency of land use. We could predict a brighter tomorrow, with larger organizations working on larger development projects, using advanced technology and improved methods of design. But the evidence before us does not indicate a technological revolution. Demand management in the homebuilding industry is primitive. We are just beginning to comprehend the potential of market control.

---

[184] Interview with Ned Eichler, General Manager of Reston, Virginia, October 3, 1967.

[185] The Editors of *House and Home,* "New Directions for the Housing Industry," in *Urban Housing* (Wheaton ed. 1966), p. 325.

[186] Kelly, "Problems and Potentials - The Housing Industry Today," in *Design and Production of Houses* (Kelly ed. 1969), p. 29.

[187] Eichler, *The Community Builders* (1967), p. 146.

[188] Herzog, "Structural Changes in the Homebuilding Industry," in *Urban Housing* (Wheaton ed. 1966), p. 322.

[189] "The Housing Market and How it Will Grow," *Business Week* (May 1, 1967), p. 92.

[190] The Editors of *House and Home,* "New Directions for the Housing Industry," in *Urban Housing* (Wheaton ed. 1966), p. 325.

[191] "The Housing Market and How it Will Grow," *Business Week* (May 1, 1967), p. 92.

[192] "New Town," *House & Home* (June, 1966), p. 95.

[193] Fact Sheets, Alcoa Properties, Inc., April 1967.

references/footnotes

[194] "The Housing Market and How it Will Grow," *Business Week* (May 1, 1967), p. 98.

[195] Blake, "Cape Kennedy," in *Architectural Forum* (January-February 1967), p. 54.

[196] Eichler, *The Community Builders* (1967), p. 146.

[197] Interview with Donald Shapiro, Levitt & Sons, Inc., Lake Success, N.Y., November 18, 1967.

[198] Kelly, "Problems and Potentials — The Housing Industry Today," in *The Design and Production of Houses* (Kelly ed. 1959), p. 43.

[199] "Five Ways to Cut the Cost of Land Development," in *House and Home* (September 1964), pp. 70-76.

[200] Bailey, "The City Meets the Space Age," in *Architectural Forum* (January - February 1967), p. 60.

[201] *The States and Urban Problems* (Commission on State - Urban Relations, National Governors' Conference, October 1967), p. 56-57.

[202] Blake, "Cape Kennedy," in *Architectural Forum* (January - February 1967), p. 59.

[203] "The Housing Market and How it Will Grow," *Business Week* (May 1, 1967), p. 15.

[204] *Ibid.*, p. 99.

[205] Katz, *Design of the Housing Site* (1966), p. 9.

[206] "Riis Plaza: Three Acres Filled With Life," in *Architectural Forum* (July 1966), pp. 68-70.

[207] "How to Plan the Land to Produce Better Communities," in *House and Home* (September 1964), p.52.

[208] Planned unit development is a vague term. The editors of the University of Pennsylvania Law Review have declared that in its simplest form a planned unit development is a project containing "a number of homes of the same type combined with common open space." For a complete discussion of planned unit development, see "Symposium: Planned Unit Development," 114 University of Pennsylvania Law Review (1966).

[209] *The States and Urban Problems* (Commission on State - Urban Relations, National Governors' Conference, October 1967), pp.72-73.

[210] "How To Plan The Land To Produce Better Communities," in *House and Home* (Sept. 1964), p. 58.

[211] *Ibid.*

[212] Boyd, "Habitat Cluster and After," in *Architectural Forum* (May 1967), p. 34.

[213] "Building with Boxes," in *Architectural Forum* (April 1968), p. 85.

[214] Bacon, *Design of Cities* (1967), p. 250.

[215] Wolf Von Eckardt, *The New Republic* (Dec. 9, 1967), p. 23.

[216] James W. Rouse, testifying on HR 12946, March 25, 1966 (emphasis added).

[217] *House and Home* (Sept. 1964), p. 48.

[218] Galbraith, *The New Industrial State* (1967), p. 208.

[219] "A New Technological Era Arrives and the Nation is Searching for its Meaning," *New York Times* (January 6, 1969), p. 147.

[220] Allan T. Demaree, "What Business Wants from President Nixon," *Fortune* (February 1969), pp. 84-85.

[221] Martin Meyerson, *"Urban Policy: Reforming Reform,"* *Daedalus* (Fall 1968), p. 1418.

Chapter 6

PROBLEMS OF LAND ASSEMBLY

In-City Land Assembly

Large parts of our cities are run-down and unattractive. They are characterized by mixed land use patterns. In many areas vacant lots and parking lots are the only "open space." With the exceptions of midtown Manhattan, the Loop in Chicago and the centers of a few other big cities, the outlook for older central cities is grim. Private redevelopment programs have been limited in the past 30 years.

White, middle-class America has shifted to suburbia for living, shopping and, in many cases, working. This has had a devastating effect on the old "downtown." Shops, offices and industry have headed for the suburbs. As the well-to-do have moved out, the poor have moved in, with blight and decay close on their heels. Major policy changes at federal, state and local levels are imperative if private investment in the central city is to be encouraged, deterioration to be checked and cities to be revived.

Land in the Marketplace

Our old cities were built up on a lot-by-lot basis. There was little need for assembling parcels of land larger than a single block. Rockefeller Center, one of the first larger-than-a-block central city developments, did not come along until the 1930's. Caught up in the shift toward suburban growth, developers have neglected central cities. This attitude might be reversed if central city development sites could be made available with a minimum of time and red tape.

In the absence of effective land assembly techniques, there are many obstacles facing the developer assembling "in-city" land. The first is price. An acre in a prime downtown location may demand hundreds of thousands of dollars. But, beyond the economics of real estate, holdouts are the most difficult factor. There are two types of holdouts.

The first, and perhaps the easiest to deal with, is the owner who simply demands more money. He has the developer "over a barrel." He wants "ransom." Either he gets it, or the project is built around him, or it is cancelled. Holdout costs of this type cannot be measured in terms of the amount of "ransom" alone. Negotiations eat up valuable time and legal fees. The developer must pay taxes on idle property already assembled. Interest and other carrying charges continue. Developers typically are action-oriented. They want to build, to get projects completed. If "locked in" by the holdout, the developer will abandon the in-city project and seek other opportunities.

The second type of holdout is the landowner who refuses or is unable to sell at any price. Once a developer knows a parcel cannot be acquired, he is faced with two alternatives. He can abandon the project, or he can attempt to work around the unavailable site. Both prospects are discouraging and expensive. One example occurred in the Foggy Bottom section in Washington, D.C. George Washington University acquired an entire block, with the exception of a one-half interest in a single house. The owner refused to sell. It took the University nearly 15 years to acquire the site and complete the development.[222]

Land economist Marion Clawson pointed out that a single holdout can encumber a whole project. He said the holdout is probably the biggest single problem of in-city land assembly.[223] In his article, "Urban Renewal in the Year 2000," he suggested legislation that would permit the private developer to use powers of eminent domain to acquire the remaining land in a given area if he has already acquired 80 percent of the tract.

The same suggestion has been made by others. The problems encountered in assembling land for a bank expansion and an apartment complex in downtown Denver were typical.[224] Assembly at the beginning was "deceptively smooth." Most owners were glad to cooperate, and wanted only fair prices. Then the holdout problem cropped up.

One block, for example, was thought to be "buttoned up." The owner of a single key lot had agreed to accept a fair price, which was in fact more than he expected to receive. Then a real estate man got to him. The owner ended up with $50,000 more than he had originally agreed to accept. The chairman of the bank involved urged an eminent domain device to handle isolated instances of speculator intervention.[225]

Fragmented ownership of land in cities is yet another problem. Many lots are small and irregular in shape. The developer who plans a large-scale project must track down and negotiate with dozens of individual owners. This is a complicated and time-consuming process.

In addition, local government creates problems for the developer with a myriad of zoning, licensing and building code restrictions frequently too complex to unravel. In the Foggy Bottom rehabilitation project, Dr. Jonas Robitscher undertook the private rehabilitation of twenty-two houses between 1953 and 1956.[226] Health, zoning and building officials were generally unsympathetic to the project, and "relations with the district government were described as difficult."[227] Frequent inspections caused costly delays. Taxes were raised immediately on improved properties, while adjacent buildings increased in value but retained low tax rates.

The difficulty of in-city land assembly is illustrated by the "parking lot technique" used by certain private developers. Dan Morgan, a Washington Post reporter, wrote a series on Washington real estate entrepreneurs Kingdom Gould and Dominic Antonelli.[228] The tale is fascinating. Picking up "a wedge here, a little lot there," the two have built an empire. Lot by lot, parcels have been purchased, the houses razed, and the land converted to parking use. Finally, as commercial expansion overtakes the once-residential area, the properties are rezoned and "a tall building sprouts on the site."

While this land assembly technique is effective, it may be

undesirable from the city's standpoint. It reduces the already low housing supply. It "cuts up" a neighborhood, destroying residential integrity, by the intrusion of small scattered parking lots. It creates intense friction between citizens and government. When rebuilding begins and the parking lots disappear, the whole process begins anew, "cutting up" the next residential neighborhood. Moreover, the technique is far from ideal for the private developer. He must contend with holdouts, the hazards of rezoning, objections from neighbors and governmental opposition. The procedure involves a long term gamble on the part of the private developer.

Assembly Under Urban Renewal Programs

There are three major problems in land assembly under urban renewal programs: (1) the selection of a site for redevelopment; (2) the lead time necessary to undertake redevelopments and (3) the relocation of families displaced by urban renewal.

All too often the sites selected are too small or otherwise unsuitable for development. "No sensible developer will build in a location where he thinks people will not want to work and live."[229] The location of the site is the principal factor in the developer's investment decision. James Appel, an urban renewal developer, put it this way, "There are three important things to consider before investing in real estate . . . These are location, location and location." A survey by his company indicated that many of the urban renewal sites were not being developed.[230] The problem is one of finding a developer who "fits" a project site; a developer whose operational size, ability and interests coincide with the projects the planners envision.

In 1960 Lyman Brownfield, General Counsel for the Housing and Home Finance Agency, declared that ". . . the total acreage of urban renewal land acquired but unsold demonstrates that the rate of disposition must be radically increased."[231] While new marketing methods have somewhat reduced the land disposition problem, it still presents difficulties for local renewal agencies.

The second major problem for the urban renewal redeveloper is the lengthy lead time required before he is able to undertake site preparation. Developers often complain of the "red tape" hang-up in urban renewal projects.[232] Condemnation procedures constitute one of the principal factors responsible for delay. Many states require negotiations for purchase prior to the initiation of condemnation proceedings. Though most land is acquired without the necessity of litigation, there are several incentives to lengthen negotiations with the agency. Among these motivating factors is the possibility of increased compensation and a tenant's desire to continue under an existing low rental agreement. Concurrently, the local renewal agency faces the major difficulty of relocating area residents and business establishments.[233]

The delay involved in the actual removal of structures in the designated project area is not, in itself, a major problem. However, it may combine with other factors to magnify their effect. A more complex situation is presented by the delay due to the establishment of unreasonably high development standards by local urban renewal directors. Edward J. Logue, former Development Administrator for Boston, and M. Justin Herman, Redevelopment Director of San Francisco, have been cited as examples of local administrators who consistently set unnecessarily high standards.[234] Such severe regulation not only discourages potential developers, but also delays the project while the plans are examined in light of complicated requirements.

Minor points are subjected to long negotiations. Several suggestions have been made as to how this delay might be reduced. For instance, the Federal Housing Administration is attempting to streamline its mortgage review procedures. What is needed, however, is the continued cooperation of federal and local agencies in simplifying the whole land disposition process.[235]

Delays tend to compound the problems. During lengthy negotiations and site clearance, unexpected pressure may develop from local citizens' groups, adjoining owners and displacees. It may take two years to plan a project, another three to prepare it for bids, and two more years to clear it. "Meanwhile, problems of clearance, increased building costs, a sagging market, a strike by one of the building trades, and a host of other frustrations may crop up."[236]

The third major problem under urban renewal programs is the relocation of families and businesses. While relocation is not the responsibility of the private developer, badly organized and poorly administered relocation procedures can lengthen the time it takes to get a project under way. Local public agencies have a statutory obligation to relocate families in decent, safe and sanitary housing, convenient to their place of work and at rents they can afford. As long ago as 1953 Jack Meltzer observed:

> To recognize the fact that relocation must inevitably accelerate competition for an already inadequate supply of housing, particularly for housing at levels that the bulk of relocatees can afford, and then to proceed with the relocation of families without providing for meeting this need is to fly in the face of reason and reality.[237]

The 1965 Advisory Commission on Intergovernmental Relations (ACIR) report, *Relocation: Unique Treatment of People and Business Displaced by Government,* stresses that ". . . the continuing shortage of decent, low-rent housing is the major obstacle to adequate relocation, with the clear implication that, despite changes in attitude, technique and services, the relocation problem will persist until the basic underlying housing problem is faced."[238] In commenting on the HHFA study of relocation, "The Housing of Relocated Families," Chester W. Hartman concluded:

> It is my belief that we will not have a satisfactory answer to the problem of relocation until improvement of housing conditions for low and moderate income families is seen as paramount, and the monies, energies, and professional talents currently available under the urban renewal program are redirected toward a different set of priorities.[239]

Under proposed new relocation regulations, where the vacancy ratio of housing in the income range affected by the urban renewal plan is less than three percent, the local public agency must demonstrate that there is comparable housing

99

available on a 1.1 basis for relocation purposes.

According to experts, increased land costs have been the most significant single factor in the increased cost of housing in California. Building costs in California, on a comparable square foot basis, have increased very little in the 10-year period from 1957 to 1967. But land costs within a commuting range of the central cities of California have doubled, on the average, in that same period of time.[240]

Suburban Land Assembly

One of the root causes of urban sprawl is the ready availability of developable land surrounding our metropolitan areas. If one has the money, land is still relatively easy to assemble outside of the urbanized area. In California, large tracts of land, originally old Spanish land grants, are still available for urbanization.[241] Several of the California "new towns" such as Irvine, Valencia and Sunset Village were built on such tracts.

Even in the East, large tracts of land are available near metropolitan areas. Robert Simon, Jr., purchased the old Bowman Estate in Fairfax County, Virginia, to build Reston. Availability of land in that particular location may have been a white elephant for Simon, however, as it was not located in the path of urbanization. According to one analysis, Reston was "too far out" for the Washington market.[242] Wolf Von Eckardt observed that Reston's rough economic sledding was also due to other factors, such as "the newness of the place," higher design costs, and the lack of long-term investment capital or "patient money."[243] Slow public acceptance probably resulted from a number of these factors, but location undoubtedly was a significant contributor.

With effort, money and luck a developer can still pull together a large tract of land, James W. Rouse of the Rouse Company in Baltimore, for example, was able to assemble land for Columbia in the urbanizing corridor between Washington and Baltimore. In the six-month period between April and October of 1963, Rouse dealt with 328 individual owners and completed over 140 separate purchases. Some fifteen thousand acres were obtained at an average cost of $1,450 per acre.[244]

Levitt & Sons' real estate manager, Don Shapiro, says that

problems involved in land assembly are part of doing business, and are not of insurmountable difficulty. He noted that Mr. Levitt himself was fond of saying that "land is nails." In other words, land is just another part of the homebuilder's raw material.[245]

These "nails" can become quite expensive items, however. "[L]and speculation tends to price single homes out of the market . . . According to the latest statistics available, the proportion of land costs to total production costs rose from 10% in 1950 to 23% in 1962."[246]

The assembly of many parcels of land held in separate ownership is one of the most "perplexing and important" tasks confronting the large-scale developer.[247] Major builders develop extensive files on available land, and are in constant communication with real estate brokers in many parts of the country.[248] Once a potential development site is chosen, the cloak-and-dagger tactics necessary for the actual assembly process are almost beyond belief. "The story of Rouse's negotiations with landowners . . . reads like a James Bond novel — secret rooms, plot strategy and dummy corporations characterized the process."[249]

The success of the land assembly program for Columbia was indeed remarkable. To date, however, it has still not been completed. According to project director William E. Finley, there are several holdouts involving key acreage. In addition, it was possible to purchase several parcels only by permitting the occupants to retain life estates in the properties. If Columbia develops as rapidly as it may, these factors could create serious future problems.[250] The comprehensive plans cannot be carried to completion while holdouts and life tenants control scattered parcels in the heart of the project.

The total cost of the land assembly program for Columbia was $23 million. The size of the project made it possible to preserve over 3,000 acres of meadow, and to provide a separate right-of-way for the public transportation system. Several million dollars are being invested in man-made lakes. Rouse paid as much as $75,000 an acre to purchase "ugly commercial islands" along US 29, in order to create a five-mile landscaped parkway through

101

the center of the new community. Spread over the cost of the entire project, these amenities added only a small amount per acre to total land cost. According to Rouse, "A developer of a few hundred, or even a few thousand acres, could not have assumed this burden."[251]

Don Shapiro observed that the use of dummy corporations and front men is common practice, even in the assembly of smaller sites. The secrecy is designed to prevent speculator intervention as well as to reduce holdouts among the original owners. Levitt & Sons recently completed the assembly of a 2,000-acre site.[252] It was initiated in late 1963 with the purchase of a fairly large tract for $1,600 an acre. At the conclusion of the assembly program in late 1967, as much as $4,500 an acre was being paid and the average per acre cost was approximately $2,500.

In addition to raw land cost, the developer also is faced with an annual carrying charge of perhaps ten percent during the assembly process. Taxes must be paid on the idle property. Interest charges on the money tied up in land are also an important factor. Many prospective medium-sized builders have failed under the burden of these various capital outlays.

Another example of difficulties of land assembly and site design is found in the development of a "new town" in Amherst, New York. Amherst, a community of 80,000 people, is planning for a new state university campus for 45,000 students to be located in the township. To meet the projected population increase of 40% the town adopted a five-year development plan which designates 2,000 acres in the northeast section as a site for a "satellite" new town. The site was selected primarily because it was located at the intersection of two major expressways planned by the state.[253]

In cooperation with local and state governmental agencies, New Smith Development Corp. announced plans in April to construct a $125 million project on a 1,200-acre tract within the designated site. The project plan was prepared by Victor Gruen Associates, a firm which had gained national recognition for its work on Valencia and El Dorado Hills, two new towns in California. The plan calls for 700 acres of single-family homes,

300 acres of garden apartments and town houses and 260 acres of restricted business locations that would include "village centers" within the new town.[254] In conjunction with this project New Smith announced plans for a golf course, covering 150 acres, to be designed by Robert Trent Jones.

Land assembly began in late February of 1967. New Smith tried to keep its land acquisition program a secret by using a number of real estate firms as purchasing agents. Don Grieco, President of New Smith, says that such efforts were not extremely successful. After the first 3 or 4 months land prices had risen from $1100 to $2500 an acre. At the present time nearly 1,000 acres of the 1,260 acres needed for the project have been assembled. In the latter stages of this acquisition program land costs had risen to over $4,000 an acre.[255]

Developer Grieco stressed the importance of timing as a factor in the land assembly process. With a land investment of over $2,000,000, carrying charges (interest, taxes, etc.) can become a significant item of project costs. Holdouts also plague New Smith. One landowner who had recently purchased a 4-acre tract with a home on the site for $20,000 is demanding $100,000 for the excess land. Mr. Grieco said that, though a desire for profit is to be expected, he considered this price totally unreasonable. He noted that some of the farm land on the site, originally purchased 10 years ago for $50 an acre, had been sold to his firm for $4,000 an acre (an 80 to 1 profit margin) but he felt that a per acre price of 6 times that amount was exorbitant. Fortunately, New Smith is able to continue its planned construction without the land in question.[256]

The large-scale commercial developer is also confronted with land assembly problems. The common practice today is to buy up available sites five or six years ahead of anticipated need. In addition, the developer often purchases several hundred acres to protect a potential commercial site requiring only a fraction of that figure.[257] Then he sits back to wait for urbanization to catch up with his acquisition. The costs of capital tie-up, interest and taxes continue to mount. Hopefully, the long term gamble will pay off.

There is every indication that the problems of large-scale land assembly will become more acute. For instance, General Electric recently announced a desire to construct an entire city for a population of 100,000 or more. The land requirements for this project are exacting. General Electric wants a minimum of 10,000 acres, within one hour's commuting distance of a metropolitan center of at least one million people. The land must be within thirty minutes of a jetport, and have access to other transportation facilities as well. For this land, General Electric will pay no more than $2,000 an acre.[258]

Needless to say, the availability of such sites anywhere in the United States is extremely limited. The requirements, however, are not unrealistic. They must be met if large corporations, like General Electric, are to be attracted to community building.

Governmental Frictions in Suburban Assembly

The most critical governmental friction in suburban land assembly is zoning. Zoning is a major problem, particularly in the eastern states. Based on his experience in assembling land for Levitt & Sons, Donald Shapiro observed that in New Jersey, "It may take three to four years of intense pressure to get a necessary zoning change."[259] If large-scale development is to take place in suburban and rural areas, some means must be found to overcome local zoning resistance.

One large company, in its "Checklist For Final Site Selection," devotes considerable attention to the local government situation. Particular attention is paid to the zoning and building regulations where the company specifically requests its investigator to determine the difficulty of altering such code requirements which may affect the project. For this company, the local government situation is one of the *primary factors* in site selection.[260]

In describing the land acquisition process for Columbia, James W. Rouse said, "Most remarkable — and perhaps most important of all: We obtained our zoning."[261] After the land had been assembled, and all the plans completed, the creation of a "new town" zoning reclassification was left in the hands of the people of Howard County. Fortunately, they bought it. Unfortunately, other developers have not fared so well. Zoning changes for large-scale development, according to Rouse, are

104

usually met with "skepticism, anxiety and perhaps a touch of hostility."[262]

The complexity of the zoning problem is immense. Zoning is one of the treasured home rule powers of local government. In the New York metropolitan area, builders must contend with "509 separate city and town zoning ordinances within 50 miles of Times Square."[263] Yet local zoning usually fails to do its job. Rouse said, "As a matter of fact, zoning has become almost a guarantee of sprawl rather than protection against it."[264]

Fundamentally, zoning provides inconsistent, localized controls for problems that are metropolitan in scope. One solution offered is to ". . . recapture from towns and counties the right to zone and return that right to the states or to metropolitan government structures."[265] Zoning expert Richard Babcock predicts that restrictive local zoning practices may be broken down in the courts, based on a new "metropolitan focus" in judicial attitudes involving land use control conflicts.[266] Even if Babcock is right, however, the judicial process is too uncertain to overcome existing zoning hindrances to large-scale, well-planned new development.

Local tax structures can also retard development. New communities and large-scale subdivisions usually do not pay their own way in terms of roads, sewers, police and fire protection, and other urban necessities. Schools in particular present a problem. New developments attract younger family groups with an over-balance of school-age children. Long time residents, anticipating rapidly increasing tax rates, ". . . stand up in the town hall and fight to keep the private developer out."[267] This is especially true in states such as New Jersey, where the tax structure is focused on small municipalities which receive little financial support from the county or state. In this situation, high potential local tax rates may drive the developer to more suitable tax climates. In general, ". . . the smaller the government body, the harder it is to deal with them."[268]

Fractionated government is a third source of friction. According to one estimate, "There are some 18,442 local jurisdictions in the 212 standard metropolitan areas of the United States."[269] It is practically impossible to plan a large-scale development that doesn't cross the boundaries of two or more sewer, fire, school or other special districts, if not municipal boundaries themselves. Conflicting objectives at these lower levels of government impede new development that would benefit the area as a whole. As these problems become more evident, ". . . the trend toward more and more state and federal participation in metropolitan affairs — both in financing and in decision-making — seems irreversible."[270]

Fractional government was a problem in the planning of the Amherst "new town" by New Smith Development Corporation.[271] The entire project was planned in coordination with town and state governmental officials. The site was part of an expanded sewer district[272] and located near a planned major highway intersection. A zoning map conforming to the project plan was adopted by town officials.[273] Yet within this coordinated planning approach, difficulties arose. The local school board claimed total ignorance of the planned community. School Trustee William Munson asked, "How can you discuss a planned community without making provision for schools?" He declared, "We want the town to do something so that the school district is not forced to pay speculators' prices for school sites."[274]

At the same time the Williamsville Central Citizens Advisory Council asked the town board to approve no subdivisions unless the subdivider provides an acceptable school site. A representative of the town replied that the proposal was "not feasible and probably not legal," especially in the case of small subdivisions.[275]

The transition, however, will be difficult. Local governments jealously guard their powers of home rule, and are loathe to part with any in favor of state or federal bureaucracy. What is needed is a regional form of government that can cope with large-scale problems and policies *without* sacrificing local control.

Summary

The private developer faces major problems in the assembly of land. In the city, a holdout may tie up a private project which could benefit the entire community. Needed urban renewal projects are delayed by protracted litigation and complicated administrative procedures. Outside of the central city, the land assembly process is characterized by secrecy and intrigue to prevent speculator intervention and holdouts. It is costly and time-consuming. In both situations the developer is confronted with the problems of dealing with local governmental agencies on zoning and subdivision regulation.

In the central city we must find a mechanism which will insure the ready marketability of renewal land and prevent unnecessary delay in needed projects. In suburban areas, a land assembly mechanism could be used to control the pattern of urban development. Location and design controls might be instituted in exchange for assembling land for development.

---

[222] Interview with William E. Finley, Columbia, Maryland, Dec. 21, 1967.

[223] Interview with Marion Clawson, Resources for the Future, Washington, D.C., December 11, 1967.

[224] Brooks, "Assembling Real Estate Without Condemnation," in *Urban Land Institute* (T.B. 54, 1965, Downtown Denver), p. 35.

[225] *Ibid.*

[226] Nash, *Residential Rehabilitation: Private Profits and Public Purposes* (1959), p. 16.

[227] *Ibid.*, p. 20.

[228] Congressional Record (March 25, 1966), pp. 6493-98.

[229] Kay, "The Third Force in Urban Renewal," in *Fortune* (October 1964), p. 130.

[230] Appel, *Urban Renewal in Private Enterprise* (1962), p. 42.

[231] Brownfield, "The Disposition Problem in Urban Renewal," *25 Law and Contemporary Problems* (1960), p. 740.

[232] Interview with Donald Shapiro, Levitt and Sons, Inc., Lake Success, N.Y., November 18, 1967.

[233] Sogg, "Legal and Governmental Issues in Urban Renewal," in *Urban Renewal: The Record and the Controversy* (Wilson ed. 1966), p. 155.

[234] Interview with Ned Eichler, General Manager, Reston Development Corporation, Tuesday, Oct. 3, 1967.

[235] Brownfield, "The Disposition Problem in Urban Renewal," *25 Law and Contemporary Problems* (1960), p. 763.

[236] Abrams, *The City is the Frontier* (1965), p. 103.

references/footnotes

[237] Meltzer, "Relocation of Families Displaced in Urban Development: Experience in Chicago," in *Urban Development: Problems & Practices* (Woodbury ed. 1953), p. 452.

[238] *Urban Renewal: The Record and the Controversy* (Wilson ed. 1966), p. 357.

[239] *Ibid.*, p. 358.

[240] John W. Dyckman, "Artichokes, Brussel Sprouts and Wine," *Hearings Before the National Commission on Urban Problems,* Volume 2, June-July 1967, Los Angeles, San Francisco (U.S. Government Printing Office, February 1968. Library of Congress No. 68-60024), p. 146.

[241] Interview with Marshall Kaplan, Gans & Kahn, Planning Consultants, San Francisco, California, Dec. 10, 1967.

[242] Bailey, "Only in Columbia, The Next America," in *Architectural Forum* (Nov. 1967), p. 43.

[243] Wolf Von Eckardt, "Are We Being En-Gulfed?" in *The New Republic* (Dec. 9, 1967), p. 21.

[244] Eichler, *The Community Builders* (1967), p. 61.

[245] Interview with Donald Shapiro, Levitt & Sons, Inc., Lake Success, New York, Nov. 17, 1967.

[246] *Harpers* (May 1968), p. 30.

[247] Interview with Ned Eichler, General Manager, Reston Development Corp., October 10, 1967.

[248] Interview with Donald Shapiro. Mr. Shapiro noted that Levitt was continually receiving offers of land available throughout the country.

[249] Eichler, *The Community Builders* (1967), p. 61.

[250] Interview with William E. Finley, Project Director of Columbia, Maryland, Dec. 21, 1967.

[251] J.W. Rouse, in testimony before the Housing Subcommittee, House Banking and Currency Committee on HR 12946, March 25, 1966.

[252] The location of the site was given as somewhere in Maryland.

[253] "Town Unveils Master Plan," *Buffalo Courier Express* (April 17, 1968), p. 41.

[254] "$125 Million New Town Project Planned for North East Amherst," *Buffalo Evening News,* (April 12, 1968), p. 33.

[255] Interview with Don A. Grieco, President of New Smith Development Corp., May 8, 1968, Amherst, New York.

[256] *Ibid.* Mr. Grieco also noted that holdouts in land designated for commercial purposes represented perhaps an even more difficult problem but he was unable to discuss the matter at this time.

[257] Interview with William E. Finley, Project Director of Columbia, Maryland, December 21, 1967.

[258] "The Housing Market and How it Will Grow," in *Business Week* (May 1, 1967), p. 94.

[259] Interview with Donald Shapiro, Real Estate Manager, Levitt & Sons, Inc., Lake Success, New York, Nov. 17, 1967.

[260] The source of this statement must remain confidential. The "Checklist" was made available with the understanding that it would not be specifically noted in the present study.

[261] James W. Rouse, testifying before the Housing Subcommittee, House Banking and Currency Committee on HR 12946, March 25, 1966.

[262] *Ibid.*

[263] *House and Home* (September 1964), p. 44.

[264] James W. Rouse, testifying before the Housing Subcommittee, House Banking and Currency Committee on HR 12946, March 25, 1966.

[265] *House and Home* (September 1964), p. 45.

[266] Babcock, *The Zoning Game* (1966), p. 174-77.

[267] Interview with Donald Shapiro, Real Estate Manager, Levitt & Sons, Inc., Lake Success, New York, Nov. 17, 1967.

[268] *Ibid.*

[269] "Census of Governments," *Local Government in Metropolitan Areas* (1962), p. 1.

[270] *Ibid.*

[271] See Suburban Land Assembly section describing the Amherst "new town" project.

[272] "$125 Million New Town Project Planned for North East Amherst," *Buffalo Evening News* (April 12, 1968).

[273] "Town Unveils Master Plan," *Buffalo Courier Express*, April 17, 1968.

[274] "School Board Claims Ignorance of Amherst Plan," *Buffalo Evening News*, April 18, 1968.

[275] *Ibid.* Statement attributed to Town Supervisor Harry R. Jones.

Chapter 7

RECOMMENDATIONS: HOW WE MIGHT IMPLEMENT OUR NATIONAL POLICIES

The National Land Commission

It might appear to be a contradiction in terms to call for the preservation of local initiative and state responsibility through the creation of a National Land Commission, but the problems of urban development and growth transcend state and local jurisdictional boundaries. These problems must be recognized and solved. The uncoordinated efforts of 50 states and several thousand local governmental agencies cannot adequately finance such an effort, nor can they implement a program which reflects the broad national implications of regional actions. On the other hand, the answer should not be a national program with a top-heavy bureaucracy, which fails to reflect local needs and objectives. As Peter Drucker warns, "There is mounting evidence that government is big rather than strong; that it is fat and flabby rather than powerful; that it costs a great deal but does not achieve much."[276] Yet at the same time Drucker also emphasizes that, ". . . never before has strong, effective, truly performing government been needed more. We need government as the central institution that expresses the common will and the common vision, and enables each organization to make its own best contribution to society and citizen while expressing common beliefs and common values."[277] The answer lies in realistic and manageable state and local action programs encouraged by the federal government through a new limited purpose agency.

It might also seem undesirable to create a new federal agency. The proposed commission is subject to the criticism that we are proliferating agencies when efficiency demands consolidation. While the Land Commission could lead to an unnecessary duplication of certain functions of the Department of Housing and Urban Development, there are three basic reasons for recommending an independent commission.

First, the task of implementing the recommendations will require a concentrated, single-purpose effort to get the program "off the ground." An independent agency is the best place to initiate a new action program which might be "buried" in a more traditional line agency.

Second, the Department of Housing and Urban Development is oriented toward the problems of the core city. While former Secretary Robert C. Weaver made impressive efforts to expand his department's activities to include the entire urban region, the effective operational emphasis was, and continues to be, on housing and urban renewal. The "urban crisis," poverty and the ghetto are in the political and financial spotlight.

Third, if we create an independent agency, it would not be biased in favor of any particular existing program or policy. It would be able to consider the entire spectrum of national land needs. In summary, the key objective is that priority must be given to improving the quality of our urban development and the mandate of the commission's activity includes the entire range of urban land development problems.

Structure, Functions and Activities

A. *Composition of the Commission*

The members of the Commission would be appointed by the President with the advice and consent of the Senate. They should be full-time, salaried officials. The Commission would also include representatives of the following departments: HUD, Agriculture, Transportation and Interior. The primary function of these representatives would be to aid the Commission in establishing effective working relationships with their agencies.

B. *Funding*

The action programs of the Commission should be financed

by a revolving fund. It is not desirable to have the long range activities of the Commission dependent on annual congressional appropriations. An initial appropriation should be used to establish a revolving fund from which the Commission would operate. The purpose of the revolving fund is to allow regional authorities to plan long term programs. Since the regional authorities will be purchasing land to be resold to private developers, some of the money appropriated to these agencies would be returned to the Commission. The appropriation needed by the Commission to carry on its day-to-day activities should, however, be made on an annual basis.

C. Relationship to Regional Land Development Authorities

There are four key elements in the relationship between the National Land Commission and the Regional Land Development Authorities. These are: (1) the establishment of regional authorities; (2) the review of annual regional programs; (3) the review of designated regional projects; and (4) the coordination of regional land programs and policies.

1. Establishment of Regional Land Development Authorities

The Commission would aid the states in the creation of Regional Land Development Authorities. It will determine whether proposed authorities conform to federal criteria. Though some powers of the Authorities will be specified by federal legislation, no attempt should be made to designate appropriate regions. This determination should be left to the states, subject to approval by the National Commission.

2. Program Review

The regional authority would submit an annual program for approval by the Commission. Funds would be provided if it is determined that the general program proposals meet the needs of the entire urban region. Though the establishment of project priorities would be left to the regional agency, the Commission would determine whether the annual program provides for a comprehensive approach. It must deal with both core city and suburban needs. The Commission will also review the program for conformance to federally established relocation and open-occupancy criteria. This would have the great advantage of building in accountability in government through an automatic abandonment process. Instead of starting with the assumption that a specific authority is likely to be eternal, we start with more realistic assumptions. Each authority would be relatively short-lived; from the beginning it would be assumed that they would come to an end after 10 or 15 years unless specifically renewed. The national Commission should not renew the programs of any authority unless it has achieved the results that it promised when it was started. This would build in the capacity to appraise results and encourage cost effectiveness as a measure of performance.

3. Project Review

The Commission will not review most individual projects of the regional agency. Project reports would be sent to the Commission, however, and it would make appropriate recommendations when necessary. The annual funding of the regional agency should give the Commission sufficient power to control agency activities.

4. Coordination

Federal departments and agencies would be required, with certain exceptions, to furnish the Commission with periodic reports concerning proposed land acquisition, disposal and development programs.[278] The Commission should keep informed of state activities involving land development. It would then advise federal and state agencies of program conflicts, and could suggest cooperative action when feasible. The Commission should publish a periodic report outlining proposed governmental actions and programs which are in conflict.

Comparison with The British Land Commission

Though there are similarities between the British Land Commission and the proposed National Land Commission, the basic organization and emphasis differs sharply. The British Commission functions as a "national land dealing corporation." It formulates objectives and carries them out through the activities of its own agencies.

Our federal system of government, the size of our nation, and the character of our urbanization would not lend itself to such a scheme. The proposed National Land Commission would not formulate and carry out individual projects. Its function would be to provide funds and guidelines for flexible regional action. Responsibility for program initiation and implementation would remain at state, regional and local governmental levels. The Regional Land Development Authorities would be the action agencies.

The Regional Land Development Authority

Special function regional authorities and service districts have flourished in the absence of metropolitan government. The need for regional agencies to deal with areawide urban development problems has been evident for 20 or 30 years. The C.E.D. (Committee for Economic Development) noted that local government cannot efficiently deal with these problems. It declared that "the heart of our problem is the use of land and other economic resources . . . in our metropolitan areas in the most efficient manner. A regional approach is needed which provides for a regional agency to preserve open land and establish broad land use planning."[279] Edward J. Logue, chief executive officer of New York State's Urban Development Corporation and for seven years head of the Boston Redevelopment Authority, put it bluntly when he said, ". . . as long as efforts to cope with the poor are geographically confined to the central city, they are bound to fail."[280]

Voters, however, have an ideological aversion to metropolitan government. They have a tendency to polarize the metropolitan government issue in terms of extreme alternatives. They worry about the abolition of local government on one hand, and the creation of "super governments" on the other. Without falling into the metropolitan government trap, we must nevertheless conclude that a limited regional approach to urban land development problems is an absolute necessity.

Urban renewal is hindered by territorial limitations on the powers of the municipality and municipal agencies. In order to achieve renewal goals, the entire metropolitan area must be

114

considered. Although several states explicitly authorize the cooperation of renewal agencies, this is of little use when a large city is surrounded by several smaller suburban communities which carry on no renewal activities.[281] Cooperation is fine when it works — but it seldom does.

To meet the regional needs of urban development, the creation of a Regional Land Development Authority is recommended. It would be established by the state or states in which it is to operate. This participation by state government is critical to the success of the regional authority. The purpose of this agency would be the assembly of land for both private developers and public agencies in the interest of planned development for our urban regions. It would assemble land for present and future urban needs, and would release the land according to an areawide planning program.

State government has begun to show an interest in state co-ordination of urban redevelopment. An illustration of this interest is found in recent New York State legislation. In February, 1967, the state legislature passed a series of acts which created an Urban Development Corporation.[282] The agency has the power to create subsidiary corporations in various regions of the state.[283] These local agencies will be assisted by local advisory committees created by the parent agency.[284] They are also required to "work closely, consult and cooperate with local elected officials and community leaders at the earliest practicable time," and to "give primary consideration to local needs and desires . . . (and) foster local initiative and participation in connection with the planning and development of projects."[285]

The Corporation is headed by nine directors (four Department heads and five Gubernatorial appointees).[286] It has a broad legislative mandate calling for involvement in housing and recreation as well as commercial development.[287] It has the power to acquire real property through accelerated eminent domain procedures.[288] Finally, the newly created agency is funded through a revolving fund established by separate legislation.[289]

115

There are five key elements of the recommendation pertaining to the Regional Land Development Authority. These are: (a) composition, (b) funding, (c) the power of eminent domain, (d) the relationship to local and regional planning agencies, and (e) the power to overrule local land use controls.

A. Membership of the Regional Authority

The members of the authority would be nominated by local governments within the region established by state legislation, and appointed by the governor of the state. Local and regional planning agencies should be represented on an ex-officio basis.

It is not essential to have every local government represented in metropolitan areas. The state could designate larger municipalities to have permanent representation, and smaller governments could be represented on a revolving basis. The National Commission, however, must have power to review the adequacy of local representation according to federal criteria. The requirement that local representatives be appointed by the governor will insure state and local cooperation with the regional authorities.

B. Funding

The funds necessary to carry out the annual programs of the regional authorities would be provided by the National Commission. However, the state would be required to provide operational funds. There would be no financial participation by local governments. Local governments have limited financial resources. In addition, the benefits of regional projects will cut across jurisdictional boundaries. It would be far too complex to establish appropriate shares to be paid by particular municipalities. Municipalities, however, would be encouraged to coordinate their land use planning and development programs with those of the authority.

C. The Power of Eminent Domain

The regional authority must be given the power of eminent domain by the state.[290] Procedures formulated by the state for the exercise of this power must facilitate the rapid assembly of land. State requirements for prior purchase negotiations and protracted compensation litigation cause a great deal of unnecessary delay in urban renewal. It is recommended that federal legislation require the state to provide a "quick take" statute.

There are two major aspects to a quick take statute. First, title may be taken simply by filing a map and description of the area at a specified official location. Second, litigation regarding compensation takes place after the land has been acquired. Examples of quick take statues can be found in several states. For instance, under Section 1007 of the New York Public Authorities Law, the Power Authority of the State of New York is given the following powers:

1. The statute declares that the public use of the land by the authority is deemed superior to the public use in the hands of any other person, association or corporation.

2. The authority is allowed to enter on the land in order to take a survey of such land for the purpose of preparing a project plan.

3. The authority is allowed to enter upon, use and occupy such land after it files with the state supreme courts a petition for condemnation and a survey and map of the area in question.

4. The entry on and use of such land by the authority is conditioned upon its deposit with the court of a sum equal to the sum of the assessed valuation of such property.

5. Compensation for the acquired land may be negotiated by the authority or be subject to condemnation litigation proceedings.

Under the New York State Highway Law, the Superintendent of Public Works may acquire property rights in land by the preparation of a survey description and map of the property, and the filing of the survey and map in appropriate local and state offices. It also provides that the Superintendent of Public Works can settle claims for the value of property appropriated by an agreement with the individual owner, or that an action may be instituted in the State Court of Claims.[291]

The quick take statute must contain a provision permitting the court to establish a suitable date for the actual change of possession. This requirement, similar to that found in Puerto Rican legislation, would enable the court to consider such factors as the necessity of relocating persons or commercial interests displaced by the proposed project.[292] The court may also consider the possibility of transferring possession of part of the property or of giving limited rights of entry in appropriate circumstances.

This legislation might be prevented by constitutional requirements in some states, on two possible grounds. First, a state constitution may mandate a hearing to determine if the proposed use is in the public interest. Second, it may require the payment of compensation before the land is taken. The former provision is acceptable, although undesirable. It is imperative, however, that possession can be taken prior to the determination of compensation.

D. Relation to Local and Regional Planning Agencies

Development projects approved or initiated by the regional authority must be coordinated with local and regional planning programs. Merely providing for the cooperation of planning and action agencies, however, is not sufficient to insure their cooperation. Federal legislation should require that project proposals be made available to designated planning agencies. These planning agencies could make necessary recommendations for the alteration of project proposals to the regional authority and the National Commission. These recommended alterations will not be binding upon the regional authority, but will be merely advisory in nature — a point which the recommendations of Section E make explicit.

In addition, the annual report of the authority must contain the reviews of its projects by planning departments of state and local government. Hawaiian legislation requires the state planning director to submit a report to the legislature as to whether specific projects of the capital improvement budget conform to the general state plan.[293] This system has proven effective in insuring state departmental cooperation with the state planning agency.

E. Overrule of Local Land Use Controls

The regional authority must be given power to overrule local land use controls which conflict with metropolitan and regional needs. Local land use controls are instruments of the individual states. The states must be given great discretion in enacting appropriate legislation. However, the National Commission will not approve the establishment of a regional authority if the state has failed to make satisfactory provision for this power.

There is increasing awareness of the need for some device to overrule local zoning. In a study presented to a National Governors' Conference Committee, the need for zoning review above the local level was noted. "The states should foster a regional perspective in zoning practice," the report urged, and it went on to recommend that zoning powers be given to ". . . counties or metropolitan planning agencies. . . ."[294]

Private Condemnation

The following procedure is designed to provide the developer with the properties he chooses, quickly and at a predetermined price. At the same time, however, various checks have been included to ensure that the public interest will be served. The entire program is intended to strike the optimum balance between private and public needs. It will operate as follows:

1. The developer will plan his own project on the site or sites he has chosen. Regional or local governmental officials should be consulted, but this would not be required.

2. A preliminary plan will be submitted to the Regional Land Development Authority. The plan must describe the proposed project in general terms, including design objectives, population densities, housing mix, open space provisions, tentative financing and other features pertinent to the particular project. A bid price for the land and properties involved may also be submitted.

3. The regional authority will then consider the proposed project and tentatively approve or reject it within 30 days.

4. If approved, the developer will submit a detailed and comprehensive project plan to the regional authority within a specified time consistent with the size and complexity of the project.

5. The regional authority will then make a final determination regarding the proposed plan within a short, specified period. In reaching its decision, the authority may require public hearings, and will be encouraged to consult regional and local planning bodies, state and municipal officials, and boards of local governments. A maximum of 60 days is suggested for these investigations. At the conclusion of the specified period, the

authority will render a final decision approving or rejecting the proposed plan.

6. If approved, the proposed plan will immediately assume the status of a complete and final contract between the Regional Land Development Authority and the developer.

7. The authority will initiate condemnation proceedings for the properties involved. Title will be transferred to the private developer according to the contract terms.

Commentary on Private Condemnation

Private condemnation is not a new or radical proposal. Marion Clawson has recommended that private developers be given the power of eminent domain even without public agencies to act as "middlemen."[295] Under the Clawson scheme, developers would have power to condemn property only under three carefully controlled conditions. The most important of these would require that the developer already own or have under option the greater portion, perhaps 80 percent, of the total plan area.

The Clawson proposal has two limitations, however. First, there would be much more social and political opposition to such a scheme than there would be to one which gives the power to a public authority. A formal check to protect the "public interest" is more acceptable. Second, if a private developer has already assembled most of the land needed for a large-scale project, his application to have the balance condemned would be treated quickly and positively by the regional authority. This would provide the same benefits as the Clawson scheme. A proposal requiring all the land to be taken through the eminent domain process, however, should be handled much more thoroughly and carefully.

In the land assembly program for Columbia, Maryland, over 175 individual parcels were assembled. While the assembly process was remarkably efficient, there remain today several holdouts who refuse to sell. Under the recommended program, the regional authority would condemn and acquire these properties for the developer. Very little preliminary investigation would be required. If the developer had wished to condemn all 175 parcels at the beginning of the project,

120

however, the authority would have had a much more complex decision to make.

Private condemnation has actually been used to meet various needs. In some western states private logging and mining interests have been given the power of eminent domain under certain conditions. In New York State, an owner of agricultural lands may condemn drainage easements on adjacent properties by filing a petition with the Conservation Commission.[296] If approved, the Commission will condemn the requested rights and transfer them to the petitioner at the assessed value.

Many states have statutes providing for private condemnation. The "Redevelopment Companies Law" in New York is typical.[297] Under this Act, a private development company submits a proposed project plan to the municipality involved. If approved by the local comptroller and planning commission, the municipality will condemn the properties and transfer title to the development company at cost. As an incentive, property tax concessions may be granted for a period of up to twenty-five years.

Several large projects have been completed under this Act, of which Stuyvesant Town in New York City is perhaps the best known.[298] The legislation is not popular with developers, however, since (1) future sale or transfer of the property is closely restricted, (2) annual profits are limited to only six percent of the total investment costs, and (3) no land cost writedown is provided.[299]

The recommended procedure would differ from the Redevelopment Companies Act in several significant ways. It is primarily designed to maximize flexibility and workability. Specifically, the decision-making process will take place at the regional level, where it is possible to take into account comprehensive areawide criteria. When necessary, the authority will have power to write down land cost, with the loss being absorbed through federal or federal-state funding. This is not possible under the Redevelopment Companies Act. Under the recommended program, the private developer will not be discouraged by profit limitations, future sales restrictions or rent controls. The objective is to provide the Regional Land

Development Authority with maximum discretion in coordinating regional needs with private initiative and development.

Land Costs

After the private developer has selected the land needed for a project, he will submit a bid price for the land to be condemned as well as a preliminary project plan. The Regional Land Development Authority will prepare its own estimate of the land acquisition costs. If the proposed project is otherwise acceptable, the following alternatives are available:

1. The bid price will be accepted. This guarantees land cost for the developer. The regional authority must absorb any excess costs of the land acquisition;

2. The bid price will be rejected, and a more suitable price negotiated; or

3. The bid price will be rejected, and the developer will be given an option to pay the actual costs incurred in the acquisition of the land by the regional authority.

Relocation

Relocation and relocation costs would be the responsibility of the regional authority. The private developer should present an analysis of relocation problems as part of his project plan. The authority would consider relocation in its acceptance or rejection of the project plan and in determining the price to be paid by the developer for the land in question. The authority should be free to base relocation compensation on a broad range of factors such as those used in Belgium and the Netherlands today. The authority must meet urban renewal relocation standards.[300] The National Commission would determine if standards have been met. If the regional authority has not adequately fulfilled its obligations, the National Commission would then refuse to approve the authority's next annual budget. Should this occur, the authority would be forced to submit requests for funds to the National Commission on a project-by-project basis.

Land Purchase Program

The major thrust of this book is the recommendation of two

122

major land assembly programs — one based on private condemnation, the other on land purchase. Each of these programs has in-city and out-city applications as well as both short and long range planning implications. However, the private condemnation approach emphasizes in-city programs to meet immediate needs, while the land purchase program is designed to meet suburban and exurban problems on a long range basis.

In comparative terms, it is only in recent years that the federal government has become financially involved in urban development. Up to the present time, the federal commitment has been centered on central cities and slums. Long range problems of urban development, such as the need to provide open space to promote an esthetic urban environment, have been stepchildren in terms of federal dollars spent. Programs to meet these problems are criticized for their supposed middle-class values and orientation.

It should be recognized that, though priority must be given to the problems of the ghetto and the poor, it is essential to find ways to deal with the broad spectrum of urban development. We must provide effective short and long range solutions. We must think of victories to be won as well as urban battles to be fought. We must look forward to a victory in the war on poverty. This would mean the extension of the benefits of middle-class American citizenship to a larger number of citizens. If we fail to adopt programs which look to the future, a victory in the war on poverty will mean only that many people will win the opportunity to live a materially better life, but still within an inefficient and unattractive urban environment.

One of the long range answers to the problems of urban development is a comprehensive land purchase program. The program must operate both in the city as well as in exurban areas. It must adopt a full range of land purchase methods. Such a program, effectively administered at the regional level, and adequately funded, could guide urban growth by restricting disorderly and uneconomic uses of land. At the same time, it could provide land for well-planned new communities.

Existing Land Purchase Programs

Title VII of the Housing Act of 1961 provided for the initiation of a Federal Open Space Land Program.[301] Although there are more than 25 federal programs which incidentally provide funds for open space, the 1961 program is designed specifically to control urban growth and development.[302]

The legislation originally provided for grants up to 20 percent of the cost of acquiring land by state and local agencies. An additional 10 percent was provided if the land purchase was designed to meet the needs of an urban region. In 1965 this percentage was increased to a maximum of 50 percent, and the range of the program activities was extended.[303]

In the first two years of the program, 110 public agencies were assisted in the acquisition of land and over 200 applications were received from governmental bodies in 36 states. Eighteen million dollars was given to assist in the purchase of over 51,000 acres of land.[304]

Several of these grants involved intergovernmental cooperation. For instance, the city of Madison, Wisconsin, bought lands as part of a long range park and open space plan prepared by the city in cooperation with surrounding communities and with the assistance of several state agencies.[305] The Open Space Land Program has continued to expand.

> In 1965, grants in the amount of almost $11 million, covering 33,700 acres and 130 projects, were approved. Since the program's inception, 402 grants in the amount of $46.7 million assisted in the purchase of 147,000 acres of land in 247 communities in 37 states. The total cost of land acquired by local bodies was $168 million.[306]

Though the program is certainly a step in the right direction, it falls short in two critical areas. First, the provision for a percentage of cost participation by local government is not realistic. Local governments today carry a great financial burden. They are barely able to meet their most immediate and pressing needs. It is too easy for cities and counties to postpone advance land acquisition in favor of more urgent projects. Local elected officials are forced to concentrate on programs with a more immediate political payoff and to adopt a "let the future take care of itself" attitude.

Second, though the program attempts to encourage a regional approach, it does not provide the mechanics for regional activity. It is all well and good to call for local intergovernmental cooperation, but experience shows that such cooperation is the exception rather than the rule.[307] We must adopt a positive approach to regional programs by providing an agency for their implementation.

The proposed "New Communities" program was an effort to develop ". . . a direct response to the threats of continued wasteful suburban development."[308] However, this admirable proposal was made without providing realistic means for implementing its land acquisition program. Loans to state and local governments for advance land acquisition cannot effectively meet the needs of regional urban growth.

In 1965 Congress passed the Advanced Acquisition of Land Program. Under this legislation the federal government will pay reasonable interest charges on loans obtained to purchase lands up to five years in advance of the proposed construction of public facilities.[309] "In fiscal year 1967, only five applications for approximately one million dollars were filed for grant assistance."[310] There is little interest in this program for a number of reasons. It is limited to land acquired for the construction of public works and facilities, and does not apply to land needed for other public purposes. It is directed to local governments, and state agencies are not eligible for assistance. It has a five-year limitation, which is insufficient for long range planning. Finally, it can be criticized in that it does not provide for a regional approach to a regional problem.

President Johnson, in his 1966 National Heritage message to Congress, stated that "the spiraling costs of land acquisitions by the Federal government for water resource and recreational purposes is a matter of increasing concern." He called upon federal agency heads "to investigate procedures for protecting the government against artificial price spirals."[311] In a response to this request the Bureau of Outdoor Recreation in the Department of the Interior prepared a report on the increased costs of recreational land.[312] In its report it recommended a stepped-up land purchase program. It found that land prices are escalading from 5 to 10 percent annually throughout the nation. This means that, given a seven percent average annual rate of increase, land prices will double in the next ten years.[313] The need for immediately increased federal activity in coordination with state and local agencies is obvious. An accelerated program for the advance acquisition of land would provide for future land needs at a reasonable cost.

The individual states have recognized this need and enacted programs for the purchase of open space. New Jersey voters approved a "Greenacres" program in 1961 which provides for the allocations of $60 million for land acquisition. New York, in 1961, voted a $75 million bond issue for open space land purchases, and an additional $25 million was authorized in 1962.[314] Land purchase programs are also found in California, Connecticut, Maryland, Pennsylvania, Wisconsin and other states.[315] However, state governments are still unable to meet the full burden of these land acquisition activities, and a greater role for the federal government is indicated.

Large-scale government land acquisition is common in Western European countries. Sweden began its land purchase program at the beginning of the Twentieth Century. Lands were purchased from private individuals and leased back for agricultural purposes until needed for development. The Norwegian land bank system operates in much the same manner. Finland has been purchasing land on the open market for several years. England is presently involved in large-scale government activities in the land market, purchasing and disposing of land in such a manner as to control directly its national growth.

Implementation of a Land Purchase Program

Though many planners and government officials agree on the need for a land purchase program, there has been considerable disagreement as to the mechanics to be employed. Following is a description and evaulation of various methods of acquiring land.

1. Land Bank

The purchase of land by local governments or public

126

corporations with federal assistance is an old concept. Under this system, land would be acquired either by open market purchase or eminent domain procedures. It would then be leased for intermediate uses while awaiting controlled development, or it may be kept as open space.

Lawrence M. Cox, recently appointed assistant secretary for Renewal and Housing Assistance at HUD, suggested that attempts at rapid completion of urban renewal projects led to hurried and piecemeal development of in-city land. He declared that the solution to this problem was an urban land bank which would retain such land until the most efficient development use is found. Local government would then have land available for specific public and private projects at a later date.[316]

In exurban areas, John W. Reps, Professor of City and Regional Planning at Cornell University, proposes the creation of either public or mixed public-private corporations with power to both purchase and condemn land. Through an expanding federal loan and grant program, the corporations would operate in a wide belt extending well beyond the boundaries of existing cities and suburbs. The system would vary. Under one approach the corporation would:

> ... convey raw land to developers, chosen through design competitions, whose programs would include broad specifications for densities, land use mixture, and building types. Generally, however, the corporations would carry out detailed site planning, install major public improvements, and reserve specific areas for public facilities and open spaces. They would then either sell or lease the remaining improved land to private developers in units of individual lots, city blocks, or entire neighborhoods.[317]

As desirable as the Reps and Cox schemes may be in the long run, they have three basic flaws which make their functional operation very difficult in the short run: (1) the program would be very expensive to implement. Regardless of long run, revolving fund payback procedures, a program designed to purchase land in or around all of our major metropolitan areas would probably be economically prohibitive in terms of political realities and in view of other national priorities; (2) such programs would require too much government control and red tape. Extensive bureaucratic machinery at federal, state and local levels would be needed to manage leased lands; and (3) an excessive amount of land would be removed from local government tax rolls for substantial periods of time.

2. Less-Than-Fee Acquisition[318]

The acquisition of limited property rights in out-city areas to prevent development is a useful planning tool for controlling urban growth ana providing open spaces. This tool has been neglected in the U.S. Under this system, title to land would remain with the original owner. He would receive compensation for the loss of his right to develop the land as he chooses, but he would retain the freedom to use the land within specified limits.

The proponents of this approach[319] declare that the restriction of development is a positive benefit which accrues to the community, and therefore compensation should be paid to the landowner. Zoning is an attempt to control land development without the payment of compensation. In addition, zoning administration is too closely tied to local interests. If zoning were applied more rigorously to control urban growth, or provide open space, it would result in a gross injustice to the landowner.

As early as 1928 a Federal Rights in Land Act was passed to permit the National Park and Planning Commission to acquire easements for park and open space purposes.[320] Today, the acquisition of such property rights is common in many states. California, New York, Vermont and Wisconsin are among the states which have such programs. Their nature and scope varies widely from state to state. California, for instance, has been acquiring scenic easements in land adjacent to state parks since 1933. In New York the State Department of Public Works has been acquiring easements restricting the erection of billboards near controlled-access state highways.[321] Wisconsin and Ohio have used the purchase of easements to preserve highway rights-of-way. Wisconsin has also initiated a scenic easement program. There are many more examples of the use of easements by both federal and state agencies for a variety of purposes, such as flood control and airport protection.[322]

The advocates of the development rights system wish to limit the use and scope of such easements. In the late forties, England attempted to control and direct urban growth through the nationalization of development rights. It was hoped that urban growth could then be controlled through the sale of these development rights. They were eventually forced to abandon the system as unwieldy. Though wholesale condemnation of property rights is undesirable, the selective acquisition of development rights will be useful in many circumstances.[323]

The principal advantages of less-than-fee acquisition are (a) cost is reduced, (b) land is not removed from local tax rolls, (c) the landowner receives equitable treatment, and (d) valuable land does not lie idle while awaiting development.

3. Compensable Regulations

Jan Krasnowiecki and Ann Louise Strong, of the University of Pennsylvania, have devised an alternative to the purchase or condemnation of development rights. They call it "compensable regulations."[324] Under their proposal:

> The appropriate governmental unit, having determined what controls are desirable ... would map the areas involved and adopt regulations prescribing how the tract in question may be used. This map and regulations would be much the same as zoning, but instead of the covert approach of the minimum acreage requirement, these regulations would state boldly what development is permitted and what is not.[325]

The regulations would make no attempt, however, to interfere with existing uses.

There are two principal differences between compensable regulations and the acquistion of development rights. First, the proposal for compensable regulations recommends deferred, rather than immediate payment of compensation. Compensation takes the form of a governmental guarantee that, on sale of the property, the owner will receive a price equal to the value of the land prior to the imposition of controls. Second, no property rights are actually taken. The controls imposed would be similar to zoning.

Krasnowiecki and Strong argue that development rights are difficult to define without being minutely specific, thus severely restricting present uses and tending to make later readjustment difficult. They also claim that development rights are difficult to evaluate for purposes of compensation, and this may result in high acquisition costs. In addition, they note that the purchase or condemnation of development rights may involve a windfall for landowners who do not intend, or are not able, to develop their land.[326]

The alternative proposed by Krasnowiecki and Strong, however, is also subject to several criticisms. The authors specify that their system would not be employed to change existing uses. This would result in widely varying regulations from one property to the next, and would be subject to the same criticisms as spot zoning. In addition:

(a) A deferred payment system might cause the landowner to feel that his property rights are being taken without compensation;

(b) The proposal would result in either (1) immediate litigation to determine value, or (2) an extremely difficult later valuation to determine the value of the property at the time controls were imposed; and

(c) Since immediate payments are not made, the government would be forced to assume a substantial future liability of an indefinite amount.

4. Open Space Districts and Land Trusts

Private associations have been formed in a few small, high-priced developments for the preservation of open space.[327] Developers use restrictive convenants and easements to achieve this objective. Restrictions are placed in the deed, and the property is sold to individual landowners. They then form private associations to carry on the open space preservation and maintenance program. A land trust is essentially the same thing, except that the initiative comes from an association of private citizens rather than a developer and relies on state tax laws for effectuation. A land trust is a private non-profit corporation organized by local citizens for the purpose of receiving gifts of land and managing them. Because trusts are devoted to educational, scientific and charitable work, their holdings are exempt from property taxes. Contributions to a trust are tax-deductible. If the trust can also demonstrate that it

130

is a "publicly supported organization" (by IRS standards), donors of land or money can enjoy an extra 10 percent charitable deduction and carry-over.

There are some 25 trusts in Connecticut, but none in New Jersey because New Jersey's tax structure has, so far, frustrated conservationists who want to get trusts started there. There is no provision for tax abatement on land held by a trust in New Jersey.

Connecticut land trusts have, at last count, managed to save some 4,000 acres for prime open space. Most were gifts but, in some cases, the trusts have raised money to buy land. These systems are limited because they are hit-and-miss and because of the difficulty of privately administering a program for large developments.

Another device has been adopted by the city of Los Angeles. Essentially, it involves the use of a special assessment district to preserve open spaces. These districts are formed by petition of the majority of individual landowners in a particular area. They submit to the levy of a special assessment for the preservation and maintenance of selected open space areas by local government agencies.[328]

There are two severe limitations to all three of these devices. First, they rely on private individuals to establish each program. There are no governmental incentives to encourage the private initiation of open space districts or associations. Second, they cannot adequately meet regional needs since their range and effect is local.

Recommended: A Comprehensive Program

1. *In-City*

The Regional Land Development Authority, in cooperation with city and county government, should purchase vacant or abandoned city land on the open market. This land could be purchased for a variety of purposes including parks, playgrounds and possibly off-street parking in residential areas. In addition, city land could be purchased to meet long term development requirements, although this aspect of the program should be limited.

The in-city land purchase program must be limited in scale to

131

prevent a substantial weakening of the real property tax base. Emphasis must be placed on close cooperation with local government.[329] Land held by the Regional Land Development Authority should be managed and maintained by and for the benefit of the municipality in which the land is located.

2. Suburban

The Regional Land Development Authority, in cooperation with regional and local planning agencies, could purchase land to meet open space and recreational needs of local government. Land necessary for future industrial or other large-scale development schemes could also be acquired. Finally, the authority would provide assistance in the formation of private open space associations and, where feasible, special assessment districts.

3. Rural

The greatest emphasis of the comprehensive land purchase program must be placed on the purchase of development rights or other less-than-fee property interests in rural areas. This aspect of the program is an essential ingredient in the long range control of urban development. It is the least costly method of protecting land needed for future open space and recreational needs. It would provide another method for controlling urban sprawl, and a device for state and local government to channel urban growth.

The accusation that development rights are extremely difficult to evaluate for purposes of compensation is without merit. It is difficult to value any property that does not have a ready market, yet such valuations have been accomplished for a number of years. William H. Whyte, Jr., has found that there is little evidence to support the contention that an easement will cost as much as the outright purchase of land.[330]

The program would operate as follows: (a) Land would be acquired primarily through negotiated purchases, although eminent domain procedures would be available if necessary; (b) new development could take place only upon the sale of the appropriate property rights by the regional authority; (c) sale of property rights by the regional authority would require prior approval from the regional planning agency for the proposed development.

What Would an Effective Land Assembly Program Cost?

While a precise estimate for a comprehensive land purchase program is impossible, indications are that an effective program could be initiated for a relatively modest amount, especially when compared with the enormously large amounts of money usually needed to fund federal urban programs. In the first few years, relatively few states would be responsive; therefore, the amount needed to fund Regional Land Authorities would be limited to those states which had adequate enabling legislation and to those areas which had organized Regional Land Authorities. Moreover, as the program continues in time, it would become self-sustaining through the amounts paid back from private developers and realtors to the land authorities and the National Land Commission.

Additional program costs would be determined by subsequent program expansion if Congress should decide to meet the nation's recreational land needs. For an example of the scope of possible expenditures, one estimate for the tri-state New York metropolitan region alone called for 550,000 acres at a cost of $1.9 billion in 1960 prices.[331] It can readily be seen that similar programs in all metropolitan areas would produce a massive program with extremely high costs.

Land costs and needs vary from region to region. The purchase of less-than-fee property rights, however, should reduce over-all program costs substantially. For example, experiences in Wisconsin in the early 1950's indicated an average scenic easement cost of fifteen dollars an acre. Ohio has acquired easements at a cost as low as five dollars an acre, and the acquisition of air easements near a Naval Air Station in California ran fifteen dollars per acre. All of these prices were substantially below the cost of an outright purchase of the land. Generally, the indications are that a substantial saving may be had.[332]

In summary, the program recommended here must be tailored to meet the specific needs of the individual area or region. Each regional authority must possess a broad range of tools to accomplish its objectives. No one scheme should be used exclusively. The important aspect is that only a single agency operating at the regional level would be able to employ a variety of techniques to meet coordinated open space, new community and large-scale land development needs.

---

[276] Drucker, "The Sickness of Government," *The Public Interest* (Winter 1969), p. 3.

[277] *Ibid.*, p. 12.

[278] The activities of certain departments, such as Defense, and agencies, such as Central Intelligence, would have to be exempted from this requirement when such a report would impede their departmental functions.

[279] Committee for Economic Development, *Guiding Metropolitan Growth* (1966), pp. 4-5.

[280] John H. Fenton, "New Approaches for Cities Urged," *New York Times*, February 2, 1969, p. 61.

[281] Sogg and Werthheimer, "Legal and Governmental Issues in Urban Renewal," in *Urban Renewal: The Record and the Controversy* (Wilson ed. 1966), p. 133.

[282] N.Y. Urban Development Corp. Act, N.Y. Urban Development and Research Crop. Act, and the N.Y. Urban Development Guarantee Fund Act (1967).

[283] N.Y. Urban Development Corp. Act, § 12.

[284] N.Y. Urban Development Corp. Act, § 4 (1).

[285] N.Y. Urban Development Corp. Act, § 16.

[286] N.Y. Urban Development Corp. Act, § 4.

[287] N.Y. Urban Development Corp. Act, §§ 7,8.

[288] N.Y. Urban Development Corp. Act, § 13.

[289] N.Y. Urban Development Guarantee Fund Act (1967).

[290] The grant must be accompanied by a definition of the scope of the power of eminent domain which will allow the agency to assemble land in an effort to solve a broad range of urban problems.

[291] N.Y. Highway Law, § 29.

[292] Thus the relocation plans of the regional authority would be subject to review by the courts, as well as a general review by the National Commission in its examination of the authority's annual program.

[293] Hawaii Rev. Laws, § 98F-4 (Supp. 1963).

[294] The complete text of this recommendation, as reprinted in the Congressional Record — House, H17271 (daily ed. Dec. 15, 1967), is as follows:

references/footnotes

States should act more energetically in recognition of their responsibilities for proper land use and should not be content to delegate unconditionally all zoning authority to localities; there should be procedures by which alleged abuses of zoning might be reviewed above the local level, not limited to the courts in the first instance. The states should foster a regional perspective in zoning practice by the development of a state land use plan or regional plans, with procedures for obtaining conformance to such plans; and, where necessary to promote sound growth patterns, states should give zoning powers to counties or metropolitan planning agencies or should provide municipalities with extraterritorial zoning powers, especially with regard to unincorporated areas beyond their boundaries. boundaries.

[295] Clawson, "Urban Renewal in 2000," *34 Journal of the American Institute of Planners* (May 1968), p. 176.

[296] N.Y. Conservation Law, § 575.

[297] Enacted in 1942, this law was found for 20 years in N.Y. Unconsolidated Laws, §§ 3401-26. In 1962 it was transferred to N.Y. Private Housing Finance Law, §§ 100-25.

[298] For a brief analysis of the Stuyvesant Town story, see Abrams, *The City is the Frontier* (1965), pp. 95-98.

[299] *Ibid.*

[300] Urban renewal relocation standards should be mandated. That is, included within plan review must be a survey and analysis of the present housing situation covering income ranges, location, and accessibility to various population groups (e.g., white and non-white). Further provision must be made for assistance to displaced residents in finding comparable housing. At present, urban renewal programs which displace persons and businesses allow, with 100 percent federal reimbursement, for moving expenses up to certain limits. A holdout often "holds out" merely because of the probable expense of relocating. No private development, just as no urban renewal program, should be allowed to displace residents if there is no comparable housing into which they can move, and this housing should be standard. A new requirement scheduled to come into effect in regard to urban renewal programs should also apply here. This, according to Mr. James Banks of HUD, would require a city in which the vacancy ratio is less than 3 percent (which is very common during these times of housing shortage) to show that relocation housing is available on a 1:1 basis.

[301] Housing Act of 1961, 75 Stat. 183, 42 U.S.C., § 1500.

[302] Davis, "The Uses and Values of Open Space," *Yearbook of Agriculture, A Place to Live* (1963), p. 334.

[303] Dept. of Housing and Urban Development, Annual Report (1965), p. 20.

[304] Davis, "The Uses and Values of Open Space," *Yearbook of Agriculture, A Place to Live* (1963), p. 334.

[305] *Ibid.* p. 333.

[306] Dept. of Housing and Urban Development, Annual Report (1965), p. 20.

[307] As previously noted, urban renewal has provisions requiring local cost participation and intergovernmental cooperation. These provisions have resulted in serious problems for the program.

[308] Weaver, *National Land Policies,* 12 U.C.L.A. Law Rev. (1965), p. 730.

[309] Housing and Urban Development Act of 1965, § 740.

[310] Dwight R. Rettie, Director, Division of Land Development, Dept. of Housing and Urban Development, Jan. 9, 1968.

[311] *The New York Times,* Feb. 23, 1966.

[312] "Recreation Land Price Escalation," Bureau of Outdoor Recreation, Dept. of the Interior, (Jan. 1967).

[313] *Ibid.* p. 4.

[314] The New York bond issue provided more funds ($75 million) than were allocated by the federal government ($50 million) during the same period. These state bond issues require voter approval. The fact that they have been readily passed indicates that the need for open space is popularly recognized, and a program to provide it should be politically acceptable.

[315] Davis, "The Uses and Values of Open Space," *Yearbook of Agriculture, A Place to Live* (1963), p. 334.

[316] Brownfield, "The Disposition Problem in Urban Renewal," 25 *Law and Contemporary Problems* (1960), p. 760.

[317] "Bi-monthly Review of Urban America," *City* (July 1967), p. 12.

[318] Full title to property is termed a "fee simple." A less-than-fee right in property is less than full title to the land.

[319] Editors of *Fortune* Magazine, "The Exploding Metropolis" (1958), p. 131. A distinguished group of men have endorsed this development rights proposal. Included in this group were: Charles Abrams, Charles M. Haar, Edward A. Ackerman, James H. Scheuer and William H. Whyte Jr., among others. This group represents some of the most prominent names in the field of urban development.

[320] 40 U.S.C., § 72 (a), (1928).

[321] Whyte, "Securing Open Space for Urban America: Conservation Easements," *Urban Land Institute* (T.B. No. 36, December 1959), p. 12.

[322] *Ibid.* p. 14.

[323] *Ibid.* p. 7.

[324] Krasnowiecki and Strong, "Compensable Regulations for Open Space: A Means of Controlling Urban Growth," 29 *AIP Journal* (1963), p. 87.

[325] *Ibid.*

[326] *Ibid.* pp. 90-91.

[327] For a detailed description and study of these private associations, see *Urban Land Institute, The Homes Association Handbook,* (T.B. No. 50, 1964).

[328] Volpert, "Creation and Maintenance of Open Spaces in Sub-divisions: Another Approach," 12 *U.C.L.A. Law Review* (1965), p. 836.

[329] Property tax incentives can also be used to implement the land purchase program. Due to the lack of financing to purchase all the land desired, a deferred payment "land bank" system has been initiated in Norway. Under this program, the landowner is offered tax-free use of his land for 15 years. During this period, he is also relieved of taxes on profits derived from the land. After the 15 years, he is paid the sum agreed upon in the original negotiations. Profits realized on the sale of the land are tax-free. Interview with Yngvar Johnsen, Ministry of Municipal Affairs and Labor, Oslo, Norway, Oct. 15, 1967.

[330] Whyte, "Securing Open Space for Urban America: Conservation Easements," *Urban Land Institute* (T.B. No. 36, 1959), p. 30.

[331] Davis, "The Uses and Values of Open Space," *Yearbook of Agriculture, A Place to Live* (1963), p. 332.

[332] Whyte, "Securing Open Space for Urban America: Conservation Easements," *Urban Land Institute* (T.B. No. 36, 1959), p. 31.

137

Chapter 8

POLITICAL IMPLEMENTATION

Overcoming Inertia

In 1968 I was invited to speak before the annual conference of the American Society of Landscape Architects on "The Promise of Land." At this meeting I proposed the concept of a National Urban Land Policy and described the administrative machinery needed to make it effective. Later, Grady Clay, the distinguished editor of *Landscape Architecture* and an articulate spokesman for urban planning and conservation, shook his head and said, "It would be great, but I don't think the country is ready for it." He was referring to political readiness, not the condition of the urban landscape. The design professionals who have a large stake in improving the urban environment are pessimistic about the possibilities for progress, but times are changing.

We live in a period of breath-taking change. As the late Dr. J. Robert Oppenheimer said, ". . . the world alters as we walk in it, so that the years of man's life measure not some small growth or rearrangement or moderation of what was learned in childhood, but a great upheaval."[333] Yet when it comes to policy changes, the pace slows to a walk — or so it seems. When Machiavelli, the first modern political philosopher, observed that "there is nothing more difficult to change than the order of things," he was referring to policy changes. This is because, in a very real sense, one man's program is another man's policy. It all depends on one's position and perspective.

Earlier we saw that land policies, such as they are, have emerged from such vague stuff as attitudes, history and "special interest groups." The traditional concept of interest groups implies that an interest group or organization (such as the real estate lobby, developers, farmers, homebuilders, big-city mayors, conservationists, city planners or design professionals) has an obvious, unitary, self-interest in a national land policy. It implies that the interest group, or lobby, is clearly and logically aware of its special interest in a national land policy. Upon closer examination, however, the special interests of groups and organizations are multiple, pluralistic and complex because they are composed of people who have many interests, and selfish "economic determinism" is only one among many motivating factors.

The problems of formulating land policy involve so many factors that it is impossible to imagine special interest groups lining up on any side of the issue. The city planner, landscape architects, and even civil engineers, for instance, have long preached the merits of sound land use policies, but mostly they talk at each other in long-winded jargon. Long on rhetoric but short on action, particularly regarding policy, the design professionals, voting as individuals, probably represent the middle of the road, middle class point of view. Regardless of all the rhetoric and exhortation about the "Rape of the Land," the professions have not exercised any significant political initiative regarding land use practice.

Professional Shortcomings

I am singling out the design professions for two reasons. First, as a city planner, I am a member of the profession and know something about it, and second because the so-called "irresponsible" real estate lobby and land developers, homebuilders and highway lobby and other assorted "heavies" have been publicly flogged many times before. Meanwhile, the professionals have been able to practice a more ethical type of hypocrisy by talking one way in public meetings and acting another way in private practice — particularly as they serve their clients, the builders and developers.

Perhaps the major failure of the design professional is that he

139

has somehow evolved into a design "technician" — rather than a professional. The technician, as defined in this context, is one who knows everything about his job except the objectives and how he relates them to the total scheme of things. The design professions seem to have concentrated on the narrow technology of specific design projects without understanding the gross shortcomings of operating without realistic policies regarding the building of our environment. Planners, architects and engineers are also guilty of narrow concentration on blind technology. They don't seriously question the framework in which they operate. This is one of the reasons students are rejecting the old professional standards. They are more concerned with social values and the relevance of professional ethics, if found wanting. The static concept of professional practice of the past won't do for them.

The design professions have traditionally had only the vaguest concern with public policy on environmental controls. But, to paraphrase Jefferson, "Those who fail to govern themselves must suffer the government they get." Perhaps the professional should take a lesson from the urban poor, the blacks and the students and practice a little "participatory democracy."

The professional lobby is characterized by a few articulate and energetic members of the professions generally located in the Northeastern corridor — Boston to Washington — many of whom have strong ties to the line agencies such as HUD, Interior and Transportation and some 18 other Federal departments and agencies.[334] Through contracts, research grants and other ties they become extensions of the agency. The point is that the policies they push represent agency interests rather than those of architects, planners and engineers. Either they are too busy with their clients' plans, projects and programs, or they don't care.

Meanwhile, critical policy issues are left to public officials referred to as "decision-makers." Their words, mystic and charismatic, are so impressive that we often fail to analyze what their policies really mean, if anything. Their "policies" are like the "objectives" stated in university brochures. As the philosopher of University Administration, Jacques Barzun, said: " 'Objectives' are the richest crop in the world – all the virtues and the powers of man are promised, in perfect balance and vaguest language."[335] The rub comes when each of the individual agencies develops "policy." It compounds the problems of coordinating any Federal policy, if one exists.

The fact is that the agencies are becoming increasingly autonomous. They are guided by their own objectives, mostly power, and they focus on specific objectives rather than national policy. The ability of government to deliver is increasingly threatened by agency fragmentation. Larger bureaucratic empires tend to make their own working policies which, for the most part, are based on specific agency interests. They may be perfectly rational in this respect but, as a result, administrative convenience takes precedence over the public interest. When the bureaucracy determines the agenda, the objectives and the priorities, national policy becomes hypocrisy.

Oblivion in the Old-Line Agencies

The President, through the Bureau of the Budget and other administrative organizations and devices, is responsible for coordination, but the machinery is too cumbersome for any one man or even a team of experts to operate. Coordination becomes a myth. He could easily spend four years wandering around Washington, seeking coordination like a medieval knight searching for the legendary Holy Grail.

The brief history of the Office of Economic Opportunity (OEO) is useful and educating in this respect. Here a specific agency was charged with responsibility for coordinating the various regiments, battalions and companies mobilized to fight the war on poverty. Some of the units were located in the old-line agencies, such as H.E.W. and Labor. In the end, the coordination effort failed and old-line agencies absorbed the programs. Within four years it was "business as usual" for what was presented as a major social and administrative breakthrough. By 1969 Congress was eager to dismantle the poverty program, as John C. Donovan concludes in his analysis of the Federal Antipoverty Program:

Congress increasingly found it difficult to identify itself with a program it had done so little to create. Some Congressional liberals, as well as conservatives, now viewed the antipoverty program as being, on balance, a rather confusing mixture of administrative problems and political ambiguities.[336]

The disparity between the power of the agencies and anyone's capacity to coordinate or control power is fundamental to this proposal for creating new national policy and the governmental machinery to carry it out. There is a danger that, as this new agency expands, its constituency will go the way of the old-line agencies and gain a vested right to the treasury and immunity from local political direction. The critical difference with the proposal for a National Land Commission, outlined in this book, is that administrative responsibility is almost completely decentralized to regional authorities, with the administrative emphasis on local determination. Furthermore, in time, the authorities would become self-sufficient and financially independent of the National Commission.

Proposals to initiate new national policy programs are obviously a complex business. There are many approaches, but the most direct and hopefully effective is to establish a relatively informal working committee to advise the President. The President should create such a working committee to implement the recommended land assembly program. It should be charged with specific responsibility for:

1. Developing a detailed organizational study for the proposed National Land Commission and Regional Land Development Authorities. The structure, functions and interrelationships of these bodies must be clearly defined. The respective roles of federal, state and local governments must be established. The political, social and economic implications of the proposal must be assessed at each level.

2. Establishing the organizational and operational costs of the proposed program. The Federal funding function and the mechanics of the "revolving fund" aid to regional authorities must be determined. It will be necessary to distinguish between those parts of the program which will rely on outright federal grants, and those which will be implemented through the use of regional "revolving funds." The potential financial role of the state must be considered. Long term benefits of the proposed

programs should be estimated and weighed against program costs.

3. Preparing a legislative proposal for the establishment of a National Land Commission, and model state enabling legislation for the creation of Regional Land Development Authorities. A political "sounding" must be taken at each level of government. Existing programs which conflict with or overlap the proposed recommendations must be analyzed to determine the most appropriate and acceptable model for suggested state action.

4. Developing a program of public education and information regarding the value of well-planned new communities. The costs and financing of the program must be examined in detail. Consideration must be given to the mechanics of the information campaign. An evaluation must be made of the cost, use and impact of various communications media.

5. Finally, and perhaps most important, the President's working committee should be responsibile for creating a constituency for the Federal legislation necessary to create a Federal Land Commission as well as the State legislation needed to create Regional Land Development Authorities. This political recruiting campaign should include everyone from the National Association of Home Builders to the Sierra Club, divergent as their other interests might be.

The key to political implementation is leadership, and the critical skill of leadership is that of formulating a policy that a broad-based coalition of advocates and constituents can be mobilized behind. As emphasized in earlier chapters, rising expectations regarding the quality of our urban environment and the use of demand management to mobilize and direct such aspirations can create such a new constituency from a wide cross section of interest groups.

All agencies have developed a constituency of "clients." They tend to identify with and work for their clients' interests. The question of whose self-interest the agency is seeking will not be determined on an *a priori* basis. Big business — General Electric and General Motors — as well as the developers, builders, and realtors will see as much opportunity in the proposed program as the urbanologists and conservationists if skillful political leadership is exercised. Leadership should structure the program so that widely different elements of the social and economic spectrum can "buy in": the developer because it will create more business and, hopefully, profits; the advocates of the poor because it will create low-income housing.

Formulation of Policy

The need to include a wide latitude of interests in the formulation of the policy is clear. The trick is to engage the several interests into a winning coalition without compromising on over-all policy objectives. This is done through the negotiation process which is central to policy formulation. It also means identifying to new interest groups and showing them how the new policy and program will serve their ends.

In pointing out the economic advantages of the proposed land purchase program, land bank program and other advanced acquisition systems which could be implemented by the local authorities with a financial assist from The National Land Commission, it should be stressed that landowners, not developers, are reaping a great unearned profit on land today. According to the Douglas Commission report, a large share of the future increase in land values will constitute an unjustified windfall to landowners, with little benefit to the public.

In a "minority report" appended to the chapter on land-value taxation, Chairman Douglas and three other members advocate taxing "a large share" of the future increases in land values. Noting that bare land values rose from $270 billion in 1956 to $520 billion in 1966, they state:

> The owners of the land received these enormous gains without strain or effort on their parts. The progress of society created these values; the owners of the land received them . . . . Just below the surface of American life, therefore, there lies the question of whether we should allow this to happen without let or restraint, or whether we should try to take at least a portion of these socially created gains for the benefit of the society which created them.

If the increase in land values of the 1956-66 decade had been taxed at a two-fifths rate, the minority points out, "this would have produced around $60 billion of revenue."[337]

Land economist Marion Clawson takes a more moderate view. He points out that, upon closer examination, the escalation of taxes may deeply erode the economic windfall. The annual tax bite may remove a greater share of the landowners' profit than

144

the gross national estimates indicate. However, economic advantages to landowners concededly do exist, and can be valuable for the local land purchase and land bank programs. These advantages should be passed on to the public as both taxpayers and consumers. Land is one of the most rapidly rising costs for the developer, and subsequently for the builder. The price of housing can be reduced by methods and techniques designed to lower the cost of raw land.

Government land policy should rely on governmental powers rather than the purse to reduce raw land costs for well-planned developments. George M. Romney, Secretary of HUD, expressed his philosophy this way: "I happen to believe there's too much emphasis on solving [urban] problems through public money. Government's greatest role should be as stimulator, clearinghouse, and catalyst in helping release the private, independent, and voluntary sectors of the American community.[338] Whether this is the philosophy of political expediency (since Congress is loath to appropriate more money) or "creative Federalism" in a new guise is known only to Romney. But the trend is toward greater use of governmental powers to coerce or entice the private sector into the enormous task of building. The new Urban America appears to be continuing unabated regardless of political persuasion.

U.S.-Canadian Commission Reports

Perhaps the most critical factor needed for implementation of proposed new programs in a modern democracy is a broad recognition of the problem. While recognition of land assembly as an issue of national importance is hardly widespread, it has been "identified" in official governmental studies both here and in Canada. The Douglas Commission described the problem as follows:

> The successful creation of a planned-unit development or new town depends in substantial part on the ability of the developer to acquire land quickly at a reasonable price. Fragmented land ownership, even in undeveloped areas, often makes this impossible, and developers are forced to follow the easier and less desirable path of producing small-scale, sacttered developments. It is imperative, therefore, if a more rational and desirable form of development is to occur and if property is to remain largely in

145

private ownership, that the government assist private developers in land assembly.[339]

In Canada the 1969 report of the Federal Task Force on Housing & Urban Development, Paul T. Hellyer, Chairman, also clearly identifies the problem. The so-called Hellyer Report states:

> From the point of view of cost, a prime factor must be the economies of scale. Under a system of private development, land tends to be purchased and serviced in small parcels of 25, 50 or 100 acres. A development of 300 to 500 acres is unusual; one of 3,000 such as Kanata, near Ottawa, is almost unique. And yet there can be no question but that it is more efficient to assemble land and, even more important, to service it in large tracts. A large potential development property divided artificially by ownership creates any number of problems. The owner of one piece may be anxious to proceed with development — only to find that the neighboring property, often the one through which trunk services must pass, is in the hands of a speculator holding out for even larger profits, or he is caught up in the legal haggling of a contested estate. The result is confusion, even more government regulation and restriction, and ever-rising cost.[340]

While the Douglas Commission and the Hellyer Task Force both identify the land assembly problem, their solutions fall far short of resolving the issue. When it comes to political implementation, each suggests that local government should be given responsibility for solving the problem. The Douglas Commission recommends that the state extend certain powers of eminent domain to municipalities:

> State governments [should] enact legislation authorizing local governments of general jurisdiction to use the eminent domain power for the assembly of land needed for large planned-unit developments. Such legislation should include a procedure whereby such power can be used to assist private developers to assemble land for approved development. Any such assistance should be conditioned on the conformity of the project with regional plans intended to assure the availability of housing for low and moderate-income families, and otherwise to insure that the powers are exercised in the public interest.[341]

The Hellyer Commission recommends that the federal government loan money to local government:

> The federal government should make direct loans to

municipalities or regional governments to assist them in assembling and servicing land for urban growth.[342]

The reliance on local initiative is commendable, but probably unrealistic, because it assumes that local government will take on such responsibilities. The cities are already involved in more urban programs than they can handle. The recommendations also fail to recognize the realities of urban growth dynamics. The land assembly problem often occurs in a distant rural county, characterized by "low-grade urban tissue" as Lewis Mumford once termed it, well beyond the political jurisdiction of the city with land and relocation problems. The city, which has an interest in helping private developers assemble land with its eminent domain powers, will not be able to use such powers where they may be needed most. So who needs it? In short, it is likely to be an irrelevant experience.

Kaiser Committee Recommendation

The year 1968 was a prolific period for Presidential commissions on various urban problems and disorders. In addition to the Douglas Commission Report ("Building the American City": Report of the National Commission on Urban Problems to the Congress and to the President of the United States) and the Kerner Report (The National Advisory Commission on Civil Disorders), we had the Kaiser Committee report ("A Decent Home": Report of the President's Committee on Urban Housing). According to the McGraw-Hill study prepared for the Kaiser Committee:

> Raw land represents the "fastest-rising element" of all major housing costs. In 1950 the average price for the site of a new FHA-insured one-family house was $1,035, or 12 percent of the total house price. By 1967, average site value had increased to $3,766, and represented 20 percent of total house price.[343]

The Kaiser Committee concurred with the Douglas Commission in identifying land assembly as an important consideration in determining a new national urban policy. It described the problem as follows:

> Large parcels of land are usually better sites for new housing construction than smaller ones. Scale economies in construction are possible which could not be achieved on small sites. Secondly,

the developer of a large parcel can be more creative and flexible in his site plan. In addition, the larger the site, the more likely the developer will find it economically feasible to provide community facilities like parks, recreation areas, or community centers.[344]

The Kaiser Committee's solution to the land assembly problem was remarkably direct and forthright, but probably politically unworkable. It calls for the direct federal acquisition of land by HUD to be leased for the development of subsidized housing:

> To provide suitable sites for subsidized housing, it is recommended that HUD be authorized to acquire land directly by purchase or condemnation. This land would then be leased to private or public developers who would be required to build housing and related community facilities for low and moderate-income families. Because of the great financial resources of the Federal government and its ability to use the power of condemnation, this program could be an effective vehicle for aggregating large parcels of land which otherwise could not be assembled. To make sure developments are practical, HUD should be authorized to execute long-term (up to 50-year) leases at a nominal rental equivalent to not more than 1 percent of the land acquisition costs.[345]

While it is difficult to fault this approach on the grounds of "effectiveness," it is perhaps a case of administrative "overkill." It is unrealistic because under both the Democratic and Republican administrations, Secretaries of HUD have repeatedly called for local initiative and bent over backwards to avoid charges of "federal intervention" in local affairs. Both Robert C. Weaver and George M. Romney have upheld the inviolability of local determination regarding various urban assistance programs.

The Kaiser Committee states that notice should be given and a hearing should be held prior to acquisition.[346] But it is doubtful that such a hearing alone would still the cries of "federal intervention." It is almost certain that local Congressmen would be very sensitive to direct intervention in local affairs in their districts by HUD, however well-intentioned, logical, noble and badly-needed the low-income housing might be. The direct federal intervention approach of expropriating land would have great appeal for those who say the urban crisis is so desperate that it requires fast immediate action and even direct federal intervention. But this view is not shared by a majority in Congress. The Kaiser Committee also suggests that:

HUD should be authorized to pre-empt the enforcement of state or local building codes for structures built on government-acquired land if the Secretary, after review of the plans and appropriate inspection, determines that the structures meet reasonable standards of safety and durability.[347]

Further, it recommends that HUD be authorized to pre-empt local zoning and other land use regulations when felt appropriate by HUD.

Author's Commentary

On balance, the Kaiser Committee's recommendation for direct HUD acquisition of land would probably have serious unintended consequences. It would place HUD in a position of direct contention with local interests. It would open the door for direct federal intervention in other programs and probably increased local resistance to all federal assistance, truly an unfortunate consequence. In short, the Douglas Commission is probably too weak on the land assembly issue and the Kaiser Committee is too strong. A more moderate middle-range program appears to be called for — a program which could be both effective and capable of political implementation, designed to keep the federal government in its role of providing national policy and financial assistance.

The proposal outlined in this book takes the position of maximum local initiative by utilizing governmental powers (federal policy and money, state eminent domain powers, and local regional decision-making authorities) combined with private initiative, managerial skills and capital. This means that local private interests, such as realtors, land developers and homebuilders, should have a stake in determining how the proposed Regional Land Authorities operate; including such questions as what land is selected, how it is disposed of and what constitutes a successful community for all urban people. On the public side, local planners and politicians would share an equally important role in the regional authority. This book recognizes that there is not a single public interest, but many interests, in dealing with the critical issues of Land, People and Policy.

If governmental powers such as eminent domain can be used to help private developers deliver a better product, in this case better urbanization, at a cheaper price, the political feasibility in both the social and economic context may be considerably more realistic than it appears at first examination. Again, properly structured, a winning coalition could be mobilized behind a national urban land policy and the programs need to implement it.

My reply to the skeptics is taken from de Tocqueville:

> I am tempted to believe that what we call necessary institutions are often no more than institutions to which we have grown accustomed. In matters of social constitutions, the field of possibilities is much more extensive than men living in their various societies are ready to imagine.[348]

---

[333] Quoted by Warren G. Bennis and Philip E. Slater in *The Temporary Society* (Harper & Row, Publishers, 1968) p. 53.

[334] James Reston, *The New York Times* (November 23, 1966). Mr. Reston also reported that there were 170 different Federal aid programs on the books which were financed by over 400 separate agencies, aided by 150 Washington bureaus and over 400 regional offices.

[335] Jacques Barzun, *The American University: How it Runs, Where it is Going* (Harper & Row, Publishers, New York, 1968). p.213.

[336] John C. Donovan, *The Politics of Poverty* (Pegasus division, Western Publishing Co., New York, 1967), pp. 140-41.

[337] James Bailey, "221 Ways to Save Our Cities", *The Architectural Forum* (January-February 1969), p. 72.

[338] George M. Romney, *The Architectural Forum* (January-February, 1969) p. 36.

[339] "Building the American City," Report of the National Commission on Urban Problems to the Congress and to the President of the United States, Paul H. Douglas, Chairman, 91st Congress, 1st Session, House Document No. 91-34, p. 247.

[340] Report of the Task Force on Housing and Urban Development, January 1969,

[341] "Building the American City," Report of the National Commission on Urban Problems to the Congress and to the President of the United States, Paul H.

Douglas, Chairman, 91st Congress, 1st Session, House Document No. 91-34, p. 246.

[342] Report of the Task Force on Housing and Urban Development, January 1969, Queen's Printer, Ottawa, Ontario, Catalogue No. NH61-1/1969, p. 43.

[343] The Report of the President's Committee on Urban Housing, "A Decent Home," Edgar F. Kaiser, Chairman, U.S. Government Printing Office, 1969, p. 140.

[344] *Ibid.,* p. 145.

[345] *Ibid.,* p. 146.

[346] *Ibid.,* p. 146. "Prior to the acquisition of such land, the Secretary of HUD should be required to give notice and afford an opportunity for local public hearings. Acquisition should require a prior finding by the Secretary that there was a need for housing for low and moderate-income families in that area which would not otherwise be met."

[347] Ibid., p. 147.

[348] Quoted by Bennis & Slater in *The Temporary Society* (Harper & Row, Publishers, 1968), p. 76.

Chapter 9

CONCLUSION

The major advantage of the recommended program is that it provides private industry with parcels of land adequate for building new towns. It also provides urban and regional planning agencies with a very effective method for implementing their plans, something they have not had in the past. The major liability — the expanded use of the power of eminent domain — is not politically expedient because the public has not been adequately informed regarding the advantages to the consumer of well-planned private development. Political implementation will require strong leadership and the development of a broadly-based constituency. An extensive public education and information effort will be needed to demonstrate vividly how the program would help achieve an improved urban environment.

The proposed policy and programs rest on the philosophical case that the quality of our urbanization to date is dull, dreary and uneconomic. Moreover, it destroys many natural features — trees, watercourses, hills, etc., that could be preserved in larger developments. Most critics, from Lewis Mumford to William H. Whyte, Jr., and Wolf Von Eckardt, have concluded that the character of our urban environment is a national disgrace, yet they offer few realistic alternatives. This is both the strength and weakness of the case for urban chaos or, more poetically, "The Pop Landscape." It offers a remarkably comfortable philosophical crutch. Another critic of the urban scene and author of *The Public Happiness,* August Heckscher, warns that the doctrine of rationalism, basic to planning, fails us in times of rapid change if not urban revolution. ". . . (S)uch inner peace as men gain must represent a tension among contradictions and uncertainties."[340]

Other intellectual pragmatists, such as Raymond Vernon and Edward C. Banfield of Harvard, and Melvin M. Webber of the University of California at Berkeley, declare that the case against urban sprawl is overstated. They believe the pattern of urban growth reflects the kind of life Americans want to live. But does it really? Has enough choice been provided? The Restons and Columbias were never given a fair chance. The idealistic developers fell before the money market.

The need for the development and implementation of land assembly techniques depends on an innate sense of good taste and a fundamental recognition of the inadequacies and limitations of the monotonous urban environment we are repeating again and again across the landscape. In the absence of effective areawide planning programs and techniques, we can look forward to the continued decay of the core city and the further extension of an uneconomic, spread city. With or without planning, some 18 million acres will be urbanized over the next 30 years. More specifically, as the Douglas Commission concluded:

> We have come this far in our urban civilization in a haphazard way, and the result surrounds us. We cannot afford to let our future urban growth occur in the same way. The present irrational, piecemeal approach to local regulations is retarding progress in urban development. The profusion of regulatory instruments which have developed one at a time for specific purposes cannot be added to or patched up.[341]

Local governments, with limited jurisdictions and inadequate powers and resources, will not be able to rationalize urban growth. As stressed at the outset, big business must be enticed into the urban building and rebuilding game, but private enterprise alone cannot build an attractive and efficient urban America. The "public interest" in an improved standard of urbanization will require the combined efforts of the public and private leadership.

The other advanced industrialized, urbanized nations, particularly in Western Europe, have also reached the urban crossroads but they appear to have taken a better road. They have decided that government must assist in the development of a well-planned and orderly urban environment. This decision has been most clearly expressed in the new towns of England and the satellite cities of Sweden and Finland. For the most part, these efforts have been socially and aesthetically successful, particularly when compared to the quality of our urbanization.

In this country new communities, built by private enterprise, have provided a glimpse of future possibilities. At present, however, they represent only the smallest segment of our total new development. An expanded effort will require far greater governmental enticement to business in the form of guarantees and insurances, tax benefits, subsidies, and contracts and franchises, as well as the expanded use of governmental powers.

We have now come to a point in history where fundamental policy decisions must be made. We must decide whether we want to direct our future expansion into a more rational pattern of urban development or whether we want to continue down the same dreary road. One has only to open his eyes to see the consequences of that course. He will soon realize that most of our new urban growth is shoddy and chaotic and that the case of chaos is a fleeting fashion at best. The existing environment is not immutable. In the next 35 to 40 years we will double our urban real estate, with or without adequate planning programs. But with modern planning techniques that have been proven in other countries, we can assure that the quality of the new urban real estate will be substantially improved. Moreover, with a rising gross national product, rising educational levels and rising middle-class aspirations, the public demand for a much greater investment in quality urbanization is increasing steadily. The massive *quantity* of urban growth appears certain — a self-fulfilling prophesy. The time has come to capitalize on the demand for *quality* and make that a part of the great prophesy.

154

"Some men see things as they are and say, 'Why'?
I dream things that never were and say, 'Why not'?"
             — **Robert F. Kennedy**

---

[349] August Heckscher, *The Public Happiness* (Atheneum Press, 1962).

[350] *The Architectural Forum* (January - February 1969), p. 72.

Index

A

Abercrombie, Sir Patrick, 39, 64
Abrams, Charles, 44-45, 107, 135-136
Ackerman, Edward A., 136
Advisory Commission in Inter-
  governmental Relations, 12, 99
Agriculture, Dept. of, 3, 21-22
Akron, Ohio, 14
Albuquerque, N. M., 16
Alcoa, 34, 42, 79-82
Amherst, N. Y., 102-103, 106
Amsterdam, 2
Anderson, Martin, 36-37, 44-45
Antonelli, Dominic, 96-97
Appel, James, 34, 97

B

Babcock, Richard, 105
Bailey, James, 46, 92, 108, 150
Baltimore, 16, 35, 42, 100
Banfield, Edward C., 153
Banks, James, 135
Barzun, Jacques, 141
Bennis, Warren G., 150-151
"Betterment", 49-53, 73, 144-145
Block, Joseph, 1
Boston, 13-15, 98, 140
British Land Commission, 48, 50-54, 113
Brownfield, Lyman, 97, 107, 136
Brussels, 66
Brzezinski, Zbigniew, 88
Buenos Aires, 14
Buffalo, 14
Building Act of 1965 (Norway), 55
Building Act of 1947 (Sweden), 59-60
Bureau of the Budget, 141

C

California, 100, 126, 128, 133
Cape Kennedy, 80
Central Intelligence Agency, 134
Century City, Calif., 80
Champion, George, 5
Charles Town (Charleston), S. C., 13
Chicago, 2, 14, 35, 94
Christiana Oil Corp., 79
Clawson, Marion, 27, 95, 120, 144
Clay, Grady, 138
Clear Lake City, Texas, 79
Cleveland, 2, 14
Columbia, Md., 40-42, 100-101, 104, 120,
  153
Compulsory purchase, (see eminent domain)
Concentration, 23-24
Condemnation, (See eminent domain)

Congress, 9, 31, 112, 125, 133, 141-142,
  145
Connecticut, 126, 131
Conservation, 1, 4, 9, 11, 16-19, 21, 29,
  33-34, 37, 40, 42, 56, 62, 68, 79,
  81-83, 85-86, 89-91, 94, 101, 119,
  123-133, 138-139, 143, 152, 154
Council on Urban Affairs, 2
Cox, Lawrence M., 127-128

D

Dallas, 16
de Cler, Cornelius, 76
Defense, Dept. of, 134
Demand management, 77, 85-89, 91, 143
Demaree, Allan T., 12, 93
Denver, 95-96
de Tocqueville, 150
Detroit, 14
Development rights, 7, 9, 11, 117, 128-130,
  132-134
Dickinson, Robert E., 14
Dispersal, 23-24
Donovan, John, 141-142
Douglas, Paul H., 144-147, 149, 153
Downs, Anthony, 22-26, 28
Drickey, Richard A., 79
Drucker, Peter F., 7, 110
Dyckman, John W., 45, 108

E

Economic Development Administration,
  Dept. of Commerce, 3
Economics of Scale, 77-79, 81-82, 91
Eichler, Ned, 78, 83, 92, 107
Eisenhower, Dwight D., 37
El Dorado Hills, Calif., 102
Eminent domain, 5-6, 8-11, 15, 39, 48-56,
  58-61, 64, 66-69, 71-73, 95-96, 98,
  115-123, 126-127, 129-130, 132, 145,
  147, 149-150, 152
Enrichment, 23-25
Esspo, Finland, 41
Expo '67, 83
Expropriation, (See eminent domain)
Expropriation Act of 1946 (Norway), 55
Expropriation Act of 1917 (Sweden), 75

F

Farsta, Sweden, 40, 59
Federal Housing Administration (FHA),
  78, 98, 147
Federal Task Force on Housing and
  Urban Development (Canada), 146
Fenton, John H., 134

Finley, William E., 101, 107-108
Foggy Bottom, Washington, D. C., 95-96
Ford Foundation, 32
Fort Worth, Texas, 16
Freeman, Orville L., 21
Fremont, Calif., 86-87
Fuller, R. Buckminster, 80

G

Galbraith, J. Kenneth, 87
Galveston, Texas, 15
Gates, Paul, 27
General Electric, 42, 79, 104, 143
General Motors, 85-86, 143
Goldston, Eli, 6
Goodyear Tire & Rubber Co., 42
Gould, Kingdom, 96-97
"Greenbelts", 38, 40-41, 57, 62
Greer, Guy, 30
Grieco, Don, 103, 108
Gross national product, 17, 87, 154
Gruen, Victor, 102
Gulf Oil Corporation, 43

H

Haar, Charles M., 44, 138
Habitat, 83, 92
Hansen, Alvin, 30
Hartman, Chester W., 99
Hawaii, 118
Health, Education and Welfare,
    Dept. of, 3, 21-22, 141
Heap, Desmond, 73
Heckscher, August, 153
Hellyer, Paul T., 146
Helsinki, 2, 65
Herman, M. Justin, 98
Hickman, Leon E., 34
Holdouts, 7, 10, 17, 95-97, 101, 103,
    106-108, 120, 122
Home rule, 105-107
Homestead Act of 1862, 13
Housing, 3-6, 9, 15-19, 21-26, 30-32,
    34-38, 40-43, 47-51, 53, 55-58, 61-65,
    68-72, 77-88, 91, 96-106, 111-113, 115,
    117, 119, 122-124, 127, 131,
    139, 143, 147-148, 153
Housing Act of 1949, 12, 30-31, 36
Housing Act of 1959, 31
Housing Act of 1961, 124-125
Housing Act of 1968, 4
Housing and Home Finance Agency
    41, 97, 99
Housing and Urban Development,
    Dept. of, 3, 5, 21, 31, 36, 41, 45,
    81-82, 111, 135-136, 140,
    145, 148-149
Houston, 15, 79
Howard, Ebenezer, 38
Humble Oil & Refining Co., 42, 79
Humphrey, Hubert H., 21

Huxtable, Ada Louise, 29

I

Illinois, 30
Integration, 23-26, 112-113
Interior, Dept. of, 3, 111, 125, 140
Irvine, Calif., 41-42, 100

J

Jefferson, Thomas, 4, 13, 140
Jim Walter Corp., 79
Johnsen, Yngvar, 136-137
Johnson, Lady Bird (Mrs. Lyndon B.), 89
Johnson, Lyndon B., 4, 43, 125
Jones, Harry R., 109
Jones, Robert Trent, 103

K

Kaiser, Edgar F., 147-149, 151
Kaiser Industries, 42, 79
Kanata, Ontario (Canada), 146
Kansas City, 16
Kaplan, Marshall, 108
Kennedy, Senator Edward M., 21, 37
Kennedy, Robert F., 155
Kerner, Otto, 147
Krasnowiecki, Jan, 129-130

L

Labor, Dept. of, 21, 141
Laguna Niguel (Calif.), 42
Land Authority (Puerto Rico), 72-73
Leapfrogging, 16-17
Letchworth (U. K.), 38-39, 42-43
Levittown, 78
Lichfield, Nathaniel, 53
Lindblom, Olavi, 64-65
Logue, Edward J., 98, 114
London, 14, 38-39
Los Angeles, 2, 14-16, 42, 131
Lundin, Folke, 75

M

Machiavelli, 138
Madison, Wis., 124
Maryland, 41, 126
Mass production, 77-80, 83, 91
McGraw-Hill, 147
McKissick, Floyd B., 21-22
Meltzer, Jack, 99
Meyerson, Martin, 82, 90
Miami, 35
Model Cities, 1, 22, 36
Montreal, 83
Morgan, Dan, 96-97
Moscow, 14
Moynihan, Daniel Patrick, 1
Mumford, Lewis, 64, 147, 152
Munson, William, 106

157

N

National Advisory Commission on
Civil Disorders, 147
National Aeronautics and Space
Administration (NASA), 80
National Association of Home Builders
of the U. S., 43, 81, 86, 143
National Commission on Urban
Problems, 144, 147
National Land Commission, 8-9, 110-114,
116, 118-119, 122-123, 134,
142, 144
Neely, J. C., 81-82
Newark, N. J., 32-33
New Brunswick, N. J., 34
New communities (new towns), 4, 6-7,
21-22, 30, 37-43, 47, 51, 53-54, 57,
59, 62, 79-80, 85, 87-88, 100-105,
120, 123, 125, 134, 143, 152-154
New Jersey, 81, 83, 105, 126, 131
New Orleans, 15, 35
Newport, R. I., 13
New Smith Development Corp., 102-103,
106
New Towns Act (U. K.), 39
New York City, 2, 13-14, 34, 81-82, 94,
105, 121, 133
New York State, 30, 121, 126, 128
New York State Urban Development
Corporation, 114-115
New York Times, 12, 28, 37, 45, 93,
136, 150
Nixon, Richard M., 2, 90
Non-enrichment, 23
North Carolina, 21

O

Office of Economic Opportunity, 141
Ohio, 41, 128, 133
Open space, (See conservation)
Oppenheimer, J. Robert, 138
Oregon, 19
Oslo, 2, 56-58

P

Paris, 14
Paterson, N. J., 17
Pennsylvania, 126
Penn Central Company, 79
Percy, Sen. Charles H., 21
Perloff, Harvey S., v
Philadelphia, 13, 16, 84
Phoenix, 16
Pickard, Jerome, 14
Pittsburgh, 14, 81
Planned Unit Development, 82-84, 86-87, 92
Planning, 3-11, 16-19, 21-22, 26, 30-41,
47-71, 77, 80, 82-83, 85-87, 97-98,
102-106, 114-128, 132, 138-140,
145, 149-150, 152-154

Pollution, (See conservation)
Pomeroy, Hugh, 16
Port of New York Authority, 9
Portland, Oregon, 15
Potter, Roy W., 86-87
Poverty, 2, 3, 5, 16, 22-26, 29-32,
35-37, 43, 65, 82, 88-89, 94, 99, 111,
114, 123, 135, 140-144, 153
Power Authority of the State
of New York, 117
President's Committee on Urban
Housing, 147-149, 151
Public Works and Economic Development
Act of 1965, 3
Puerto Rico, 72-73, 117

Q

"Quick take" condemnation, 48, 52, 60,
66-67, 73, 117-118, 120, 122
Quota system, 24

R

Radburn, N.J., 41
Rancho California (Calif.), 79
Reconstruction Act of 1946 (Norway), 55
Recreation, (See conservation)
Regional Land Development Authorities,
8-11, 112-116, 118-120,
122, 125, 131, 133-134, 142-144, 149
Rehabilitation, 31, 35-37
Relocation, 30, 32-33, 35, 37, 55, 69-70,
97-100, 112-113, 117, 122, 135,
147
Reps, John W., 127-128
Reston, James, 150
Reston, Va., 40, 42-43, 85, 91, 100, 153
Rettie, Dwight R., 136
Robitscher, Jonas, 96
Rockefeller Center, 94
Rochester, N.Y., 14
Romney, George M., 5, 145, 148, 150
Roper, Elmo, 37
Rouse, James W., 85, 100-102, 104-105

S

Safdie Moshe, 83
San Diego, 14, 16
San Francisco, 14-15, 98
San Simeon, Calif., 42
Santa Clara, Calif., 83
Scheuer, James H., 136
Seattle, 15
Segregation, 23-24
Seip, Jens, 74
Shanghai, 14
Shapiro, Donald, 92, 100-102, 107
Sierra Club, 143
Simon, Robert, Jr., 43, 46, 100
Slater, Philip E., 150-151
Slayton, William L., 21, 44-45

Soul City, 21
Standard Metropolitan
  Statistical Areas (SMSA), 9, 105-106
Standard Oil Co. of N. J., 42
Stein, Clarence S., 64
Stevens, William K., 45
Stockholm, 2, 40, 47-48, 58-64
Strada, Ltd., 58
Strong, Ann Louise, 129-130
Stuyvesant Town, 30, 121
Subdivision regulations, 20, 47, 107
Sunset International Petroleum Co., 79
Sunset Village (Calif.), 100

T

Tacoma, Wash., 15
Tapiola, Finland, 41, 47
Task Force on Housing, (See Federal Task
  Force, et al.)
"Tax damage", 70
Thomas, Wyndham, 53, 73
Tofte, Ingvar, 74
Tokyo, 14
Toledo, Ohio, 14
Town and Country Planning
  Act of 1947 (U. K.), 48-50
Transportation, 3, 9, 15-18, 29, 37-38, 40,
  42-43, 57-58, 61-63, 83-86,
  100-101, 104, 106, 128
Transportation, Dept. of, 3, 111, 140
Twentieth Century Fox, 79

U

United States Constitution, 4
Urban crisis, 1-2, 5, 25, 29, 30, 88,
  90, 111, 123, 149
Urban Land Institute, 83, 136
Urban Redevelopment Act of 1966, 43
Urban renewal, 2, 6-8, 29-37, 60, 62, 95,
  97-100, 107, 111, 114, 117,
  122, 135, 150
Urban sprawl, 4, 11, 16-17, 29, 37, 41,
  100, 105, 132, 153-154
U. S. Plywood Co., 79

V

Valencia, Calif., 100, 102
Vallingby (Sweden), 40, 59
Venturi, Robert, 29
Vermont, 128
Vernon, Raymond, 27, 153
Veterans Administration (VA), 78
Von Eckardt, Wolf, 92, 100, 152

W

Washington, D. C., 14, 16, 42, 95-96, 100,
  140-141
Washington Post, 96-97
Weaver, Robert C., 31, 111, 136, 148
Webber, Melvin M., 153
Weinberg, Lawrence J., 80
Wells, Sir Henry, 51-52, 73-74
Welwyn (U. K.), 39
Westinghouse Electric Co., 79
West Los Angeles, Calif., 79
Wheaton, William L. C., 41
White racism, 22, 25-26
Whyte, William, H. Jr., 16, 27, 132,
  136-137, 152
Winnick, Louis, 32
Wisconsin, 41, 126, 128, 133
Wunge, Lars, 74

Z

Zeckendorff, William, 34
Zoning, 20, 32, 47, 55, 57, 59-60,
  69, 83, 85, 87, 96-97, 104-107,
  115, 119, 128-130

GORDON EDWARDS

BIOGRAPHICAL SKETCH

Gordon Edwards is director for the Office of Urban Affairs at the State University of New York, Buffalo, N.Y. He is a member of the American Institute of Planners and a planning commissioner for the town of Amherst, N.Y. He has served as consultant to the New York State Constitutional Convention, the President's Commission on Urban Problems and the United States Agency for International Development in Brazil.

He was formerly senior planner for the Federal Aviation Agency. In this capacity he was responsible for developing a systems approach for planning the nation's airport system. He received the FAA's Sustained Superior Performance award for this effort. He also served as Chief of Metropolitan Planning for the Housing and Home Finance Agency, now the Department of Housing and Urban Development, where he participated in the development of the New Community legislation of 1964.

From 1960 to 1962 he was senior planner for San Diego County, Calif. His work led to the implementation of an over-all comprehensive planning program. He also developed the first 701 planning program in the state of Oregon. Mr. Edwards received his Master of City Planning degree from Harvard University and was a Fulbright scholar in India. He has taught urban planning at San Diego State College, Catholic University of America, the American University and the State University of New York at Buffalo.